CRAIG FEAR, NTP

Copyright © 2017 by Craig Fear

All rights reserved. No part of this book may be reproduced in any form without permission in writing from the author. Reviewers may quote brief passages in reviews.

Publishing services provided by

ISBN-13: 978-1545435878

ISBN-10: 1545435871

Disclaimer

The information in this book is for educational and informational purposes only and is not intended as a substitute for the medical advice of a licensed physician. I am not a medical doctor, and any advice I give is based on my own experience. As such, you should always seek the advice of your own healthcare professionals before acting on anything I publish or recommend. By reading this book, you agree that my company and I are not responsible for your health or the health of your dependents. Any statements or claims about the possible health benefits conferred by any foods have not been evaluated by the Food and Drug Administration and are therefore not intended to diagnose, treat, cure, or prevent any disease.

Contents

Introduction 1

Part I: The Six Thai Soup Secrets 5

Chapter 1: Thai Soup Secret #1: Real Broths Are the Key 7

Chapter 2: Thai Soup Secret #2: Thai Broths Are Simple to Make 13

Chapter 3: Thai Soup Secret #3: Thai Soups Are Good for Your Gut 17

Chapter 4: Thai Soup Secret #4: Thai Soup Ingredients Are Easy to Find 21

Chapter 5: Thai Soup Secret #5: You Determine the Final Flavor 31

Chapter 6: Thai Soup Secret #6: White Rice and Sugar Have Benefits 35

Part II: Recipes 43

Chapter 7: Bone Broths: The Building Blocks of Thai Soups 45

Chapter 8: Thai Drinking Broths: Simple Medicinal Recipes for Gut Health 59

Chapter 9: Thai Congees: Restorative Rice Soups for Breakfast 69

Chapter 10: Classic Thai Soups: Tom Yum, Tom Kha, and Beyond 83

Chapter 11: Thai Fusion Soups: Fun and Creative Inspirations From Around the World 129

Acknowledgments 159

Endnotes 161

To Abigail + Stephen,

Happy Soup making!

Best Wishes,

Craig Fern

Introduction

HOW I CAME TO WRITE THIS BOOK

Life can be delightfully serendipitous sometimes. I never would've thought that my first trip to Thailand seventeen years ago would lead to a book on Thai soups. Food was not the intention of my trip. But it's hard not to fall in love with Thai food when you're in Thailand. *Especially* the soups. Because, unlike in America, soups are an everyday part of Thai cuisine—including breakfast. They're such an integral part of the fabric of life that it's hard to miss them. You see them on the streets, in people's homes, markets, cafes, restaurants, and even the Buddhist monasteries.

During that first trip, I didn't know or even care about the health benefits of Thai soups. All I knew was that they tasted amazing. It wasn't until years later, when I became a certified Nutritional Therapy Practitioner, that I learned about the healing power of *real* broths and soups. I looked back on my travels and all the incredible traditional soups I had with a newfound understanding. And so, when I returned to Thailand years later, I was ready. Everywhere I went, I ate as many different types of soups as I could, observed how they were made, photographed them, asked questions, took notes, and even signed up for cooking classes.

WHO THIS BOOK CAN HELP

I've written this book with two types of people in mind. First and foremost, I've written this book for *my* people. I started realizing that there was this tremendous untapped potential of Thai soups to help my people. Because my people need *a lot* of help. Who are my people?

My people live in the suburbs and cities of America. This is where I'm from (Long Island, to be exact). My people are crazy busy these days. They're mothers and fathers, students, single folks, husbands and wives, and they have jobs, kids, mortgages, school loans, and car payments. And they don't have a lot of time to cook. Even worse, many don't know *how* to cook. The craziness of modern life has cut the cord of connection to our cooking traditions. Most of my people, including me, have grown up on sugary breakfast cereal, bologna sandwiches, frozen pizza, fast food, and all manner of processed junk food. As a result, millions are struggling with chronic health conditions and looking for answers. The good news is that more and more of my people are waking up and realizing how toxic our food system has become. More are becoming interested in learning not just how to cook but how to cook healthy, nutrient-dense food, the way our grandmothers and great-grandmothers used to.

In a strange way, Thai soups can offer a lot of help to my people.

THAI SOUPS ARE HEALTHY AND HEALING

Probably the biggest reason Thai soups can help my people is that they are so very healthy and healing to the body. All of the recipes in this book are gluten- and dairy-free with all sorts of anti-inflammatory herbs, spices, and seasonings. In the coming chapters, I'll explain a little more about these foods' incredible health benefits. Of course, you wouldn't realize that Thai food can be nutritious from eating in most American Thai restaurants—these establishments may give you the impression that all Thai people eat is pad thai, greasy fried rice, and overly sweet and heavy coconut curries.

This may be shocking to hear, but there are *no* coconut curries in this book! Now, I love a good coconut curry as much as anyone, but please understand that they're really not soups. They're more of a rich, coconut milk–based stew. Furthermore, most coconut curries are made with commercial curry pastes that are full of chemicals, preservatives, and artificial flavorings that lack the wonderful aromas and flavors of a freshly made curry paste. In this book, fresh ingredients—with their healing properties intact—will be emphasized. And while you could certainly learn to make your own curry paste, it's a very complicated, time-consuming process. I'd wager that 99 percent of my people don't want to spend an hour in their kitchen pounding a bunch of spices into a paste with a mortar and pestle.

THAI SOUPS ARE BROTH-BASED

Unlike coconut curries, the recipes here are mostly broth-based, as broths are an essential foundation of any healthy soup recipe, be it from Thailand or another country. They're also a key part of the health protocols I utilize with clients, especially those with digestive-health issues. You'll learn about the health benefits of bone broths shortly, and don't worry—they're ridiculously easy to make.

THAI SOUPS ARE SIMPLE TO MAKE

A lot of Thai cuisine can be very time-consuming with many in-depth, highly refined, and specific techniques. Like making a curry paste. Or carving vegetables into flower shapes. (Seriously, that's a big thing in Thailand). But broth-based Thai soups are perhaps one of the simpler aspects of Thai cuisine, and I've purposefully chosen recipes that are not overly complicated. Some may involve a little more time than others, but there's nothing here that any home cook couldn't easily make.

NOT ALL THAI SOUPS ARE SPICY

Generally speaking, my people don't love hot and spicy food. But the fact is, contrary to popular belief, not all Thai food is spicy, including the soups. In fact, there are even native Thai people who don't like spicy foods. Many Thai soups are completely devoid of the intense heat of chiles. Of course, some do contain them. But here's the key: Thai soups are *always* customizable to each individual's tastes. If you don't like hot and spicy, it's not a problem. If you do like spicy, it's also not a problem. The recipes in this book that utilize chiles can be altered to your personal liking either by including more chiles, fewer chiles, or no chiles at all.

MY RECIPES DO NOT CALL FOR EXOTIC, DIFFICULT-TO-FIND INGREDIENTS

Thanks to the popularity of Thai cuisine in America, all of the ingredients in this book are relatively easy to source and access. There are no exotic ingredients; there is nothing that might shock you. I know my people can be squeamish with things like organ meats, so I don't include them. Nor are there any recipes that my people may find bizarre, like snakehead fish soup (though it is tasty) or one of my favorite Thai soups, boat noodles, which includes beef or pork blood. For better or worse, the overwhelming majority of my people are just not going to use animal blood. (I can just imagine someone going to their local supermarket and asking some teenage clerk what aisle the beef blood is in. If you want a good laugh, give it a try.)

BEYOND TOM YUM AND TOM KHA

The second type of person I wrote this book for should be pretty obvious: anyone who has a love and enthusiasm for Thai food! In particular, those who would like to learn more about Thai food in the form of Thai soups. Because, unless they've been to Thailand, most of my people can name only two Thai soups: tom yum and tom kha.

Outside of Thailand's two most famous soups, very few Thai soups make it to the menus of Thai restaurants in the West. If a trip to Thailand is not on your agenda anytime soon, this book will be your next best option for discovering this relatively unknown aspect of Thai cuisine.

In a unique way, this book combines my years of travel, the passion for Asian broths and soups that came out of those travels, and my study as a nutritional therapist to create soups that support health and wellness. In time, I hope this book leads to more books on the broths and soups from other Asian countries. Time will tell if I can make that happen. In the meantime, I look forward to expanding your knowledge and love of Thai cuisine—*and* to helping you live a healthier life.

Enjoy!

In health,

Craig

PART I
The Six Thai Soup Secrets

Chapter 1
    Thai Soup Secret #1: Real Broths Are the Key   7

Chapter 2
    Thai Soup Secret #2: Thai Broths Are Simple to Make   13

Chapter 3
    Thai Soup Secret #3: Thai Soups Are Good for Your Gut   17

Chapter 4
    Thai Soup Secret #4: Thai Soup Ingredients Are Easy to Find   21

Chapter 5
    Thai Soup Secret #5: You Determine the Final Flavor   31

Chapter 6
    Thai Soup Secret #6: White Rice and Sugar Have Benefits   35

CHAPTER 1
Thai Soup Secret #1: Real Broths Are the Key

If you're like me, until recently, you probably had no idea what a *real* bone broth was. When I was growing up, my mother rarely made them and instead did what most full-time working mothers did in the 1970s and '80s: she used bone broth from a box or can or in the form of a bouillon cube. Convenient as they are, none of these store-bought versions are real bone broths.

Conventional store-bought broths often use monosodium glutamate (MSG) and other artificial flavorings to mimic the meaty flavor of real broth. Organic versions are not much better. They also use a variety of flavorings. These watered-down, hastily prepared versions are nothing even remotely close to the real thing.

It wasn't until 2008, after I'd suffered with chronic digestive issues for several years, that I learned there's a big difference between store-bought and homemade broths. For starters, I learned that real bone broth was a central part of almost every kitchen around the world prior to World War II. I also learned it's been used medicinally to treat a variety of illnesses. As a result, real bone broth is making a big comeback today as more and more people are rediscovering its many health benefits.

WHAT EXACTLY IS REAL BONE BROTH?

At its simplest, a real bone broth is animal bones and often other animal parts that are simmered in water for an extended time—often with vegetables, aromatic herbs, spices, and roots that infuse the water with flavor and nutrients—that is used as a base for things like sauces, stews, and, of course, soups.

Like many things in life, once you get beyond that basic definition, things can get complicated. Variations in how to make a bone broth are seemingly infinite. Ask one person and you'll get a slightly different answer from another person. Clear versus cloudy, thin versus gelatinous, and short cooking times versus long cooking times are just a few of the more common differences. Even terminologies differ.

WHAT'S THE DIFFERENCE BETWEEN A BROTH, A STOCK, AND A BONE BROTH?

For the most part, the words *broth*, *stock*, and *bone broth* are used interchangeably to describe the same thing. Generally speaking, trained chefs (mostly from European traditions) will often use the term *broth* to describe a light, short-cooked version that usually contains more meat than bones (as meat will impart a lot of flavor). They'll use this broth for a wide variety of soups. On the other hand, chefs use the term *stock* to describe a long-cooked version that contains more bones than meat (as well as other collagen-rich animal parts), which they'll use for gravies, demiglaces, and richer stews and soups. These long-cooked stocks can be simmered as long as twenty-four hours for pork and poultry bones (and even much longer for bones from larger animals, such as cows).

For reasons I'm unsure of, many health and food bloggers have started using the words *broth* and *stock* in the opposite way from culinary traditions. You'll often see the term *meat stock* used to describe what most chefs consider a broth and *bone broth* to describe what most chefs call a stock. To make things even more confusing, many now use the term *bone broth* as sort of an umbrella term for both broth and stock. But it doesn't matter what word or words you use. For the sake of simplicity, I use the words *broth* and *bone broth* in this book. Regardless what you call it, both short- and long-cooked versions have tremendous health benefits.

A BRIEF OVERVIEW OF THE HEALTH BENEFITS OF BONE BROTHS

If you've ever visited a Thai food market that includes animal products (and most do), you might be shocked at what you see. *All* parts of the animals are on display—not just different cuts of meat but collagen-rich bones, heads, backs, tails, feet, and internal organs, too. Though chefs still value and use them, these parts have mostly disappeared from our supermarkets and our home kitchens. Many Americans are even grossed out by them! But it wasn't too long ago when we lived on family farms, butchered our own animals, and used these parts. In Thailand and many other countries, they're still an everyday part of life and are highly valued for their many health-giving properties.

Bones are, of course, made of minerals and will break down and leach out in a slowly simmering broth. These minerals include not only calcium but also many other minerals that play important roles in the body, including magnesium, potassium, sodium, and many trace minerals as well.

Collagen from the collagen-rich parts will also break down in a slowly simmering broth. Collagen is the most abundant protein in mammals and makes up the pliable but strong tissues whose function is to support, cushion, bend, stretch, and connect us. In fact, collagen comes from the Greek word *kolla*, which literally means *glue*. When a broth cools, you can see evidence of the collagen in the form of gelatin (which is essentially cooked collagen). A gelatin-rich broth will jiggle just like Jell-O. Gelatin consists of about twenty different amino acids that also play essential roles in the body. Let's take a brief look at just a few health benefits.

Digestive Health

Broths are very gentle on the digestive system and help to nourish the delicate mucosal gut wall, especially if it's been damaged through modern, inflammatory diets. Minerals like magnesium have a very soothing effect on the body, and mineral-rich broths help relax muscles in the gut wall, soothe digestive discomfort, and promote regular bowel movements. The amino acid glutamine helps fuel and regenerate the lining of the small intestine and is popular in supplement form for such purposes. The amino acid glycine helps support proper stomach acid secretion and promotes good bile flow, both of which are also essential for proper digestion. Prior to World War II, many doctors understood the healing potential of gelatin and actually used it to treat a wide variety of digestive issues.

Inflammation and Immunity

Mothers and grandmothers around the world have used simple chicken soups for ages to ward off the common cold and treat various inflammatory ailments. Today, we know that bone broth contains glycine, proline, and arginine, three amino acids with anti-inflammatory effects. There was even a scientific study published in 2000 proving the anti-inflammatory and immune-boosting powers of traditional chicken soup.[1]

Joint Health

Another component of bone broths are molecules called proteoglycans, which are large, gelatinous molecules that act to lubricate and cushion our joints, muscles, and bones. Countless people take two proteoglycans in supplement form for joint health, glucosamine and chondroitin sulfates, without realizing they can get those same nutrients at a fraction of the cost in a homemade bone broth.

Skin, Hair, and Nails

Another proteoglycan, hyaluronic acid, is common in skincare products but also occurs naturally in a real bone broth. Collagen is also a component in our skin and helps give it integrity and suppleness. It does the same for our hair and nails. Many people report an improvement in previously dry, cracked, and brittle skin, hair, and nails when they start consuming collagen-rich foods.

Bone Health

You might think that the minerals in bone broth are the primary benefit to healthy bones, which, after all, are composed of minerals. Interestingly, several studies have actually shown that bone broths are not high in calcium.[2] However, broths present minerals in an easy-to-assimilate form and in proper ratios. Calcium doesn't exist in a vacuum. It needs other minerals (especially magnesium) in proper balance to function properly. Most calcium supplements do not consider these ratios. And bone is not just made of minerals. It's actually only about 50 percent minerals. It's also made of collagen, which helps keep bones strong and pliable. Therefore, a bone broth made from both bones and other animal parts provides a full spectrum of nutrients that support good bone health.

There are dozens more potential health benefits that are a bit outside the scope of this book. *Nourishing Broth* by Sally Fallon Morell and Kaayla T. Daniel, PhD, has some excellent chapters about the health benefits of bone broth if you'd like to learn more.

As far as making bone broth, don't worry—it's ridiculously easy. And that's Thai Soup Secret #2.

CHAPTER 2
Thai Soup Secret #2: Thai Broths Are Simple to Make

One of the great things about traveling in foreign countries, especially those that are vastly different from your own, is that they can open your mind and challenge many of your preconceived cultural notions. Even the most minor things (e.g., making a bone broth) can have a different approach for different reasons. As mentioned in the previous chapter, in the West, it is typically recommended to simmer bone broths for long time periods, often upward of twelve hours. This helps leach nutrients from the bones and results in a richer, more complex broth. Interestingly, this is not how it's done in Thailand.

THAI BROTHS ARE SIMMERED FOR SHORT PERIODS

A typical simmer time for Thai broths is between one and four hours, with most tending toward the shorter end of that spectrum. This short simmer time results in a fairly light and clear broth (though not always). This is because, traditionally, most Thai soups were not meant to be a whole meal by themselves but part of a larger meal with other courses. However, this is not always the case in modern Thailand, and for the purposes of this book, the recipes are intended as full meals. When you learn to make bone broths in chapter 7, I'll give you the option to make the broths as rich or light as you prefer. The differences are fairly minor and won't dramatically alter the final results of your soup.

Regardless which type of broth you choose, a shorter cooking time certainly makes the process a lot quicker and easier. Long-cooked broths often bring up some logistical concerns, as many people are not comfortable leaving their stove on overnight or when they're not home. And if you're planning on using that broth for dinner tonight, well, you'd better plan ahead. A short-cooked broth doesn't present those issues, and for most people today, that's certainly a good thing.

But that's not the only difference between Thai broths and Western ones. Let's take a look at a few more.

THAI BROTHS ARE NOT GELATINOUS

Because of their shorter simmer times, Thai broths do not develop the gelatinous quality that many Western broths do. But just because a broth is not gelatinous doesn't mean it's inferior. Broths are inherently easy to digest and, sometimes, lighter ones are easier on the body's digestive system. Furthermore, lighter broths will still contain the same nutrients as long-cooked ones, albeit in smaller concentrations. Many of those nutrients can be replaced from other ingredients in both the broth (see chapter 3) and the soup itself, such as meats and vegetables.

Another reason Thai broths tend not to be gelatinous is that larger bones from larger animals, such as cows, which inherently contain more collagen, are not commonly used in Thailand. Even Thai chickens tend to be much smaller than the big meaty birds you'll often find in other countries.

Finally, sometimes the answers to these differences are found in geography and climate. Keep in mind, Thailand is a mostly tropical country. This is just an educated guess on my part, but perhaps, prior to the advent of refrigeration (which was not that long ago), there was little use for gelatin-rich broths, as the formation of gelatin requires cool temperatures of around 60° Fahrenheit and below.

THAI BROTHS AND SOUPS ARE OFTEN MADE TOGETHER IN ONE STEP

Typically in the West, we make a bone broth first and then use that broth to make a soup later. But in Thailand, this is often done together in one step: The bones are often simmered in water with the other soup ingredients and then the bones are discarded before serving. Or sometimes those bones are meaty bones like chicken thighs or pork ribs and remain in the final soup recipe. We don't usually include bone-in cuts of meat in soups in the West, but this is very common in other countries, especially throughout Asia.

THAI BROTHS USE THAI VEGETABLES, HERBS, AND SEASONINGS

That shouldn't be shocking news. Instead of the usual Western addition of carrots, onions, and celery, Thai broths use things like lemongrass, ginger, galangal, shallots, garlic, cilantro, and other ingredients commonly used in that part of the world. This variety gives Thai broths a subtle but distinct flavor. Furthermore, many of these ingredients have their own health benefits too.

And that leads us to Thai Soup Secret #3.

CHAPTER 3
Thai Soup Secret #3: Thai Soups Are Good for Your Gut

Today, millions of people are suffering with chronic gut issues brought on by the forces of modern living. Stress, poor diet, chemical exposure, and the overuse of antibiotics and other medications can lead to all sorts of digestive issues: constipation, diarrhea, bloating, excess gas, irritable bowel syndrome (IBS), candida, and various types of intestinal inflammation, to name a few. Over time, these can lead to connected issues like weight gain, metabolic disorders, and even autoimmune issues. We are understanding more and more that the root of all health starts in the digestive system.

Most people at some point seek medical help. And while many medical treatments can be effective (and often costly), I can't tell you the number of people that come to see me who are fed up with medical treatments. They've tried everything—this procedure, that procedure, this drug, that drug. They're sick of taking drugs, few of which ever solve the underlying problems (not to mention that drugs cause all sorts of side effects). People are desperately looking for natural alternatives.

Could you imagine if your doctor said to go home and make yourself a bowl of tom yum, Thailand's most famous soup? They'd probably lose their medical license.

Before the rise of the medical and pharmaceutical industries, cultures around the world looked first to the healing properties of local herbs, spices, wild plants, roots, trees, and fruits. Every culture has its traditional folk medicine based on the local flora and fauna. Today, modern herbalists, acupuncturists, Ayurvedic practitioners, and naturopaths are just a few types of holistic practitioners that carry on these traditions. Even modern science has identified thousands of phytochemicals in herbs—such as antioxidants, phenols, and flavonoids—that have a wide range of healing properties.

Through thousands of years of trial and error and passed-down knowledge, native cultures have used the natural substances in plants to treat various illnesses. These natural medicines were administered in concentrated forms like tinctures, essential oils, salves, teas, tonics, and, of course, soups.

Soups are a wonderful medium for administering the healing power of medicinal plants. As they simmer in broth, they release their nutrients and phytochemicals, diffusing not just their health benefits but also their oils, aromas, and wonderful flavors that make them so enticing to the nose and tongue.

In America, there's probably no better example of edible medicine than chicken soup, which mothers and grandmothers have used for ages for easing indigestion and treating various digestive issues. In Thailand, tom yum and dozens more have been used for similar purposes. And dozens if not hundreds of different types of medicinal plants native to Thailand are used in these soups. But there are three in particular that I want to highlight, as we'll be using them extensively in the recipes.

THE TRIPLE GEM OF THAI SOUPS

In Buddhist countries, the Triple Gem refers to the three pillars of Buddhism: the Buddha himself, the Dhamma (the teaching of the Buddha), and the Sangha (the community of people, especially monks and nuns, that distill the teaching to others). If you've ever been to Thailand, a deeply Buddhist country, you know that these three pillars are evident in everyday life.

Now, I mean no disrespect to anyone who is devoutly Buddhist, but when it comes to Thai soups, I also feel there's another triple gem—namely, lemongrass, galangal, and kaffir lime leaves.

Lemongrass and kaffir lime leaves are highly fragrant herbs, and galangal is a highly pungent root. They are used so often together in Thai soups and are so essential to the flavor and aroma of them (and many other Thai dishes) that I also refer to them as "the triple gem." These ingredients are also highly valued by Thai people for their healing properties.

HEALTH BENEFITS OF THE TRIPLE GEM

Lemongrass is used to help digestive issues such as diarrhea, gas, constipation, stomachaches, and nausea. It's also used to help lower blood pressure, act as a diuretic, help with insomnia, alleviate pain, and ease a variety of respiratory issues.

Many of these benefits aren't just anecdotal either. Scientific studies have shown lemongrass is effective for fighting stomach infections, including *H. pylori*;[3] has potent antimicrobial effects;[4,5] has potent antifungal effects and can help fight candida;[6] can help improve insulin sensitivity and help treat type 2 diabetes;[7] benefits the immune system;[8] and supports healthy cholesterol levels.[9]

Galangal is used to stimulate appetite and digestion. It's used to soothe inflammatory issues like gastritis and ulcers, to help reduce pain, to treat fevers, and it is also used in antibacterial and antifungal applications.

Multiple clinical scientific studies confirm galangal's antimicrobial effects.[10,11] Research also shows it can help boost the immune system[12] and may even protect against stomach cancer.[13]

Kaffir lime leaves are used to aid digestion, benefit oral health, and purify the blood. The highly aromatic oils in kaffir lime leaves are used in many bodycare products, like shampoos, skincare products, insect repellents, toothpastes, and mouthwashes.

Scientific research shows kaffir lime has anticancer effects,[14,15] the ability to boost mood,[16] antimicrobial effects,[17] and it can even ward off mosquitoes.[18]

Of course, there's a lot more to medicinal Thai plants than just the triple gem. Fresh chiles, ginger, turmeric, coconut oil, cilantro, and many other Thai ingredients we'll be using in the recipes all have their own health benefits. I could go on listing them and the scientific research, but I think you get the idea.

Also, please understand that this book is not meant to treat any specific health condition. There's a lot more to healing the body than just consuming more soup. That being said, soup made from real bone broth infused with medicinal herbs and roots is an essential part of any gut-healing protocol. If you have chronic heartburn and gastroesophageal reflux disease (GERD), my first book, *The 30 Day Heartburn Solution*, lays out an extensive approach, including making your own broths and soups. Most of the recipes in this book would fit perfectly with that approach. They'd also fit with many other digestive protocols that emphasize real food and minimizing or eliminating highly processed junk food.

But even if you don't have any health issues, you'll still probably feel some benefits from making these soups on a regular basis. It could be a sense of calm and relaxation or even sleeping better. Or maybe you'll experience just a general sense of well-being and feeling nourished. Whatever the reason you've picked up this book, even if it has nothing to do with health, just know that the benefits go far beyond their many wonderful flavors.

Now, you might be asking where to find lemongrass, galangal, and kaffir lime, as well as what other ingredients you'll need for these recipes. No need to worry. That leads us to Thai Soup Secret #4.

CHAPTER 4
Thai Soup Secret #4: Thai Soup Ingredients Are Easy to Find

You might think there will be dozens of exotic, unfamiliar Thai ingredients in the recipes that appear in this cookbook. While on occasion there might be an uncommon ingredient that I encourage you to seek out, I'll always recommend substitutes in such instances. I promise you won't have to go to Thailand to find anything! In fact, there are what I consider fifteen essential Thai soup ingredients (pages 23–29), and most of them are very easy to find in Western countries. This list of fifteen essential ingredients is not an exhaustive list of every ingredient used in this book but rather the most common ones you'll see throughout the recipes and the ones most central to Thai soups. If you have these stocked in your fridge and pantry, you'll never be too far away from whipping up some incredible Thai soups.

WHERE TO FIND THAI SOUP INGREDIENTS

There are four sources where you can shop for the fifteen essential ingredients as well as other Thai foods: conventional supermarkets, health food stores, Asian markets, and online sources.

Conventional Supermarkets

Let's start with conventional supermarkets, most of which now have an Asian section. You won't find a ton of stuff here, but you can probably find some packaged products like coconut milk, fish sauce, soy sauce, jasmine rice, and rice noodles. Your choices will probably be limited to a handful of products, though, and they probably won't be great quality, either. It will also be difficult to find fresh Thai produce in conventional grocery stores.

Health Food Stores

A step up in quality and variety would be health food stores like Whole Foods, most of which also have an Asian section of packaged items. You might be able to find a few fresh items too. For example, I can almost always find lemongrass and Thai chiles in my local health food stores now, though I've yet to see fresh galangal and kaffir lime leaves.

Asian Markets

Your best choice for finding the fifteen essential ingredients in one place will definitely be an Asian food store. If you live in an urban area, there's very likely at least one (if not several) Asian markets nearby. They can be small stores or as big as a regular supermarket. Regardless the size, you'll almost certainly be able to access all of the essential fifteen Thai ingredients that follow. And you'll probably have some better choices for good-quality Thai products and fresh produce.

A word about Asian food stores: If you've never been to one, it can be a little overwhelming. You'll find a lot of unusual foods, to say the least, especially if there's an extensive produce section and meat section. But you'll also find a lot of highly processed products. You'll see MSG and a litany of other artificial flavorings, as well as artificial colorings and preservatives, in a rather high percentage of packaged goods. The middle aisles of Asian supermarkets can be as scary and unhealthy as the middle aisles of American supermarkets. But with the increasing demand for better-quality foods, there's usually some good choices too.

Online Sources

If you don't have an Asian supermarket near you and can't find some of the essential fifteen ingredients, do not despair! There are a few online sources where you can order very good quality products, including fresh produce. The best source is www.importfood.com, which is a specialty online Thai supermarket. Another good source is www.templeofthai.com.

Recommended Good-Quality Products

Sifting through all the choices—either in stores or online—can certainly be a little overwhelming. If you need help identifying good-quality items, I've created a page on my website, which you can find at www.fearlesseating.net/thai-soup-resources, with a list of recommended products.

THE FIFTEEN ESSENTIAL THAI SOUP INGREDIENTS

What follows is a short description of the fifteen essential Thai soup ingredients as well as some instructions for how to prepare them for use in soups.

Lemongrass

Lemongrass is perhaps the quintessential herb and spice in all of Southeast Asian cuisine. It is a very thin, long, and fibrous plant and has a highly pungent citrus quality that is used to infuse and flavor a wide variety of dishes. Please do *not* use lemon juice as a substitute. And please do not use dried lemongrass, which is devoid of its fresh oils and flavor. It is not hard to find fresh, whole lemongrass these days. It's sold in places like Whole Foods and specialty health food stores and can always be found in Asian supermarkets. If you don't have access to one of these places, you can find fresh lemongrass online at www.importfood.com.

Lemongrass is similar to leeks in that the stockier bottom half is the part we use. Simply slice the lemongrass stalk in half and either discard it or, better yet, save the thin green upper half for your soup broths. You'll be left with a 6- to 8-inch piece.

Next, slice about ½ inch off from the hard bottom end of the lemongrass stalk. Remove the fibrous outer layer, which will expose the more tender and pungent inner part. We'll be using this part in two ways.

For infusing broths and soups, lightly bruise the lemongrass with a meat hammer or any flat, dull kitchen utensil. This will break down the cell walls and help to release the essential oils. Then cut the stalk into about 2-inch pieces or even smaller ¼-inch thick slices. I use the former with longer simmer times (e.g., when making a broth) and the latter with shorter simmer times (e.g., when making a soup, as the smaller rings have more surface area exposed to the cooking liquid). Try to cut the ¼-inch thick slices diagonally, at a 45-degree angle (in the culinary world, this is called "on the bias"), which will create longer slices with even more surface area. These tough and fibrous pieces are not meant to be eaten and are either removed from the soup when it's ready or left in and simply avoided when consuming the soup (see page 63).

The second way to use lemongrass in these recipes will be to slice the lower half of the stalk into very thin pieces and then mince them. In this case, it's okay to eat it. Lemongrass prepared in this way usually becomes part of a paste or a mixture of other finely chopped veggies and herbs.

Galangal

Also used as an aromatic, galangal is a rhizome in the ginger family and is an integral part of many Thai soups but especially the classic soups, tom kha and tom yum. While galangal resembles ginger in appearance, it has a more citrus-like, peppery flavor. It also tends to be a bit woodier and tougher than ginger, which is also why it's ideal for using in soups. While ginger can often be substituted for galangal, it will add a different quality and flavor that's not always ideal for some recipes.

To prepare galangal, simply peel the outer skin and slice the galangal against the grain into small circles, about ⅛ to ¼ inch thick.

Kaffir Lime Leaves

Kaffir lime leaves are best used fresh and give soups a hint of lime—but they are nothing like using actual lime juice, which should not be used as a substitute. They have their own distinctive aroma and flavor that is hard to describe! These leaves are small, dark green, somewhat shiny, and grow with two leaves connected together. They are usually added to soups whole or torn into a few pieces. Galangal and kaffir lime leaves are the two ingredients that may be the hardest to find outside Asian supermarkets.

Coconut Milk and Coconut Cream

It is the full-bodied, sweet, and luscious creaminess of coconut milk that gives many Thai soups (especially tom kha) their characteristic flavor. *Always* buy full-fat coconut milk. No one in Thailand uses low-fat coconut milk. That's about as sacrilegious as using ketchup in place of tomato sauce in an Italian recipe, for instance. And to be clear, make sure to purchase real, unsweetened coconut milk in cans (or small aseptic boxes) and not the kind sold in milk-like cartons (or soy milk–like aseptic boxes) in the nondairy-milk section of supermarkets.

Coconut cream is richer and has a thicker consistency than coconut milk, as it is often added to soups to do just that: make them richer and thicker. Both coconut milk and coconut cream are made by simmering shredded coconut meat (the inner white, fleshy part of the coconut) in water. Coconut cream simply uses a higher ratio of coconut meat to water to give it a creamier consistency.

Fish Sauce and Soy Sauce

The quintessential salty seasoning sauce of Southeast Asia, fish sauce also adds a wonderfully subtle umami quality to many dishes. Good-quality fish sauces have a light brown color and are not overly fishy in taste or smell. If possible, purchase a brand from Thailand that uses only fish and salt. Avoid all products that include MSG, added sugar, and other natural or artificial flavors.

Soy sauce is not native to Thailand but has certainly migrated into Thai cuisine from neighboring cultures. Thai-style soy sauces are not as robust as soy sauces from Japan or China. Their light and mild flavor can make soy sauce interchangeable with fish sauce. I prefer fish sauce in most of these recipes and try to limit the use of soy sauce as it usually contains small amounts of wheat (thus, gluten). The one place where soy sauce does work really well is in noodle soups, which are influenced by Chinese cuisine. But if you want to avoid gluten entirely, there are gluten-free soy sauces available in stores. You can also use coconut aminos, which is a soy sauce replacement product made from the sap of coconut trees.

Limes

If not an essential ingredient in a soup recipe, limes are still included on the side as a condiment for almost all Thai soups. Please don't substitute lemons. I'll never forget the Thai restaurant I went to in Westchester, New York, many years ago. When I asked for a lime with my meal and the waiter told me they only had lemons, I knew what was about to happen. My meal was lousy. Lemons are not common in Thai cuisine.

It should also be noted that the limes native to Thailand are a bit smaller, juicier, and sweeter than the typical Persian limes sold in the United States. If you can find Key limes, often sold in conventional supermarkets, these would be the closest to Thai limes. But regular limes are not the end of the world and are fine to use. Finally, if you're going to make several of these recipes at once, be sure to stock up on a lot of limes, especially if you're making some of the sweet and sour or hot and sour soups. At a minimum, you'll need several tablespoons of fresh lime juice for the sour component.

Thai Basil

Thai basil is an herb that adds a sweet licorice flavor to soups. It has purple stems and flowers and slightly smaller, more pointed leaves to distinguish it from the more common basil of Western cuisine (also called sweet or Genovese basil). Holy basil and lemon basil are two other types of basil in Thai cuisine, but they are not as frequently used in soups. You may find Thai basil in some farmer's markets or gardening centers, as it can easily be grown at home just like sweet basil.

Cilantro

You'll find this popular worldwide herb used in countless Thai soups in a variety of ways. Also known as coriander, its roots are often pounded into pastes with other ingredients like peppercorns and garlic, but the whole plants with roots attached are almost impossible to find in US stores. The leaves and soft, crunchy stems are often added to soups as a condiment and are also used in pastes.

Palm Sugar and Coconut Sugar

Much like maple trees in the northern United States and Canada, palm trees can be tapped for their sweet sap, which can then be boiled and concentrated into sugar. This natural sugar has been used in Thai cuisine for centuries and has more flavor and nutritional benefits than refined white sugar (more on this in chapter 6). Palm sugar is often sold in a hardened form that will dissolve when added to hot soups. It has a rich, caramel-like flavor and can be found in most Asian supermarkets.

Coconut sugar is a little different than palm sugar. It comes from the buds of the flowers of the coconut tree (a type of palm tree) and is most often sold in a granulated form similar to white sugar. It has a much lighter flavor than palm sugar and is better used as a condiment to sweeten soups to taste after cooking. Coconut sugar is now widely available in all health food stores and some conventional supermarkets.

Jasmine Rice

With an aroma akin to jasmine, this soft and slightly sticky long-grain variety of rice is central to Thai cuisine and culture. It's often included in soups or as a side dish that one can pour a spoonful of soup over. Rice and rice noodles (discussed in the next paragraph) add depth and heartiness to many soups. Try to find jasmine rice grown in Thailand. All supermarkets will carry it. For the soup recipes that don't include it directly in the broth, there's always the option to simply steam or boil the rice and include it on the side.

Rice Noodles

Rice noodles are made from rice flour and water and come in many shapes and sizes. You can use any type you want, but for the most part, I use two types in this book: vermicelli rice noodles (which are very thin noodles that resemble angel hair pasta) and flat rice noodles (which resemble linguini pasta). Both types are widely available in dried form in all types of supermarkets. You'll certainly find more variety in Asian markets, though there are many poor-quality, highly processed products full of preservatives and chemicals. Look for products that are made just with rice flour. Organic is, of course, the best choice. Freshly made rice noodles are fantastic if you can find them in some Asian markets.

Coconut Oil, Palm Oil, and Lard

When making soups, it's often necessary to first simmer veggies like shallots, onions, and garlic in oil to help release their flavors. Traditionally, coconut oil, palm oil, and lard are the most common cooking fats used in Thai cuisine. Coconut oil and palm oil are widely available, though both have many environmental concerns over the way they're harvested. Check labels and only purchase a product that is harvested sustainably. Lard may be more difficult to find, though many health food stores now sell it.

These fats may be surprising to see here as they've long been demonized as unhealthy (especially lard). Nothing could be further from the truth! These are traditional cooking fats that are staples all over the world. They are extremely stable at high heat and thus ideal for cooking. For more info, please see my blog post, "Seven Reasons Why You Should Eat Lard," at http://fearlesseating.net/seven-reasons-why-you-should-eat-lard/.

While other fats and oils can be substituted for coconut oil, palm oil, and lard, many have their own strong flavors that clash with Thai food (e.g., olive oil). If you choose to use other oils, please make sure to avoid all highly processed and genetically modified industrial oils, especially canola oil, cottonseed oil, soybean oil, and corn oil. No cultures on this planet ever used these oils for food purposes prior to the twentieth century.

Garlic, Onions, Shallots, and Scallions

Alliums—such as garlic, onions, shallots, and scallions—are a genus of related flowering plants with bulbs that have a characteristic garlicky and oniony taste and smell. These are all prevalent in Thai cuisine and are used extensively in these recipes in different ways.

Ginger and Turmeric

Ginger and turmeric are both closely related and should be available in most health food stores and Asian markets. Freshness is key with both as they lose their flavor when they become dried out. Give them a squeeze in the supermarket to make sure they're nice and firm. Another good sign of freshness is a smooth outer skin. Store them in your refrigerator in plastic wrap or airtight plastic bags to keep them fresh. Young ginger is great to use if you can find it. It has a whiter flesh and pinkish-red tips. Best of all, because it's so tender, it doesn't need to be peeled.

Chiles

There are many types of chiles used in Thai cuisine, but bird's eye chiles—small, extremely hot chiles sometimes referred to as Thai chiles—are probably the most common. But more importantly, they are the variety most available in Western countries. They're about 2 inches long and come in either unripe green or ripe red colors. Generally speaking, the green ones are spicier (though heat levels can vary widely).

Be careful when using fresh bird's eye chiles! Everyone's tolerance for heat and spice is different. Simmering even just one bird's eye chile in a soup can dramatically increase the heat level. I usually recommend 1–3 chiles per recipe, though you could use a lot more than that if you really love things spicy. To tone down the heat, slice the chiles lengthwise and scrape out the seeds and some of the inner flesh. When cutting fresh bird's eye chiles (or any hot chile), be careful not to handle them (or any part of the inner flesh) with your bare hands. I made this mistake once and spent the next two hours with my burning hands submerged in ice water.

Any type of chile can be used as a substitute for bird's eye chiles, especially if you have an intolerance (or just a dislike) for heat and spiciness. The ones I commonly recommend in place of bird's eye chiles are jalapeños and serranos, both of which are often found in conventional supermarkets. Both are most often sold in their green stage, and both taste and look similar. Serranos are about 2–3 inches long and about ½ inch wide. Jalapeños are a little larger, about 3–4 inches long and about 1 inch wide. The big difference is that jalapeños are mild to moderately spicy whereas serranos tend to be hotter. Use serranos if you like and can tolerate more heat.

Dried Roasted Chile Powder

Dried roasted chiles, most often red bird's eye chiles, can be further ground into coarse flakes or a fine powder and used as a condiment. Most recipes in this book will include dried chile powder as an optional seasoning. This is one of the four classic Thai soup seasonings (more on seasonings in chapter 5). There are often several types of chile powders in stores, many of which are interchangeable, but try to find a product from Thailand if you can.

Finally, if you do have an intolerance to hot and spicy foods and are concerned about using chiles, do not worry—that is Thai Soup Secret #5.

CHAPTER 5
Thai Soup Secret #5:
You Determine the Final Flavor

One of the reasons I love Thai soups so much is that the final flavor is unique to each individual. *Recipes are guidelines, not absolutes.* Always feel free to adjust things to your personal tastes. For example, if you don't like spicy foods, not a problem—use fewer chiles, milder chiles, or no chiles at all. Thai cuisine has a reputation for being fiercely spicy, but this is not always the case. As you'll see, many of the recipes in this book are not spicy at all. Those that are can be easily altered.

But one thing that is essential to Thai cuisine is the *balancing and harmonizing* of flavors—in particular, sweet, spicy, sour, salty, umami (often defined as savory), and sometimes even bitter. Thai soups tend to use many if not all of these flavors in the form of fish sauce, soy sauce, sugar, chiles, lime juice, and various herbs and spices.

Throughout this book, you'll notice there will be ingredient lists sporting the header "Seasonings, to Taste." *You* choose which ones to employ and how much to add of each. I don't even suggest amounts. For example, if there's fish sauce listed, I don't say "2 teaspoons," because one person might want none and the next might want a heck of a lot more. It's totally up to you.

In other places, you will see a *suggested* range in the ingredients, such as "1 to 3 chiles." Start on the lower end of that range and add more, if needed. You'll know when you've hit the sweet spot (no pun intended): expressions like "Oh my God!" and "Yeah, baby!" will spontaneously roll off the lips (often with the occasional expletive).

Also, it's important to note that the freshness and quality of the ingredients you purchase will affect the flavor, thereby affecting the degree to which you season things. There can be vast differences in, say, a vegetable, herb, or fruit grown in one area of the world versus another. Soil conditions, rainfall, altitude, sunlight, the use of chemical sprays (both during and after harvest), and when the plant was picked from the vine or plucked from the field will determine its flavor profile. For example, heat levels of chiles can vary widely, even from the same type of chile. I've had jalapeños that were so spicy I could barely tolerate them and jalapeños that barely had any heat at all.

The flavor of packaged foods like fish sauce, soy sauce, dried chiles, and dried spices will also vary considerably depending on many factors. For example, not all fish sauce is the same. Most fish sauces are hastily prepared for mass consumption with chemical flavorings and preservatives. The better ones stick to age-old techniques with less processing, allowing the true natural flavors to develop over time. Thus, they're often produced in smaller batches and cost more. Quality matters! Quality food tastes better and is better for you. Always try to get the best-quality ingredients you can.

It's important to taste as you go and alter your soups to your personal preference. Sometimes my bone broths have enough flavor on their own that I don't need to add much else. Sometimes they're a little plain and I add a little more salt or fish sauce or maybe a little more heat or sweetness.

Sometimes you'll season a recipe as you're cooking the soup on the stove, and sometimes you'll do this afterward in each individual bowl. If I'm cooking for friends and family, I tend to ease up on the seasonings (especially the chiles) in the main pot and allow each person to season the soup as they desire in their own bowl. And this is certainly how it's done in Thailand.

THE FOUR QUINTESSENTIAL THAI TABLE SEASONINGS

Regardless where you travel in Thailand, you'll find a caddy of seasonings on every table in every cafe, restaurant, or street-side food stall. Although variations exist throughout the country, there are four basic ones: two fresh chile-based sauces, a sour one with vinegar and a salty one with fish sauce; dried roasted chile powder; and sugar. These four allow each person to adjust the saltiness, sweetness, sourness, and spiciness to their preference. Other common seasonings may include lime wedges, freshly sliced chiles, fried garlic, fried shallots, ground peanuts, various herbs, chili pastes, and many other types of relishes and sauces.

Fresh Chile-Based Sauces

If you're new to Thai cuisine, the two fresh chile-based sauces may seem a bit unusual; but I'd encourage you to make them at home and see how they both balance and add depths of flavor to soups. For starters, they're beyond easy to make. But they also temper the heat of fresh chiles, especially over time. In the "recipes" in the sidebar on pages 33-34, you can use any type of chile you want. I put the word "recipes" in quotes there because they're so simple, I can barely call them recipes.

It should also be noted that not all soups mesh well with chiles in fish sauce or chiles in vinegar. Generally speaking, soups that contain rice or noodles will make a better fit than soups without them. Let your intuition and your personal tastes guide you.

Roasted Dried Chile Powder

Roasted dried chile powder is readily available in both health food stores and Asian markets. It's just a simple powder—sometimes coarsely ground, sometimes finely ground—from roasted and dried red chiles. There can be several types available from different types of chiles with different heat levels. You can use any of these, but try to find a brand from Thailand that uses bird's eye chiles.

Chiles in Fish Sauce
Nam Pla Prik (or Prik Nam Pla)
Makes ½ cup

Nam pla means *fish sauce* and *prik* means *chiles*. This seasoning almost always utilizes bird's eye chiles, so it can be pretty spicy. Go easy here and add just a few chiles at a time to the fish sauce. You can also add a little lime juice, garlic, and sugar for a fancier version.

Ingredients

- ½ cup fish sauce
- 10 to 15 bird's eye chiles, thinly sliced into small rings
- 1 to 2 cloves garlic, thinly sliced (optional)
- ½ to 1 teaspoon fresh lime juice (optional)
- ½ to 1 teaspoon coconut sugar (optional)

Directions

In a medium jar with a tight-fitting lid, combine the fish sauce and bird's eye chiles. Add the garlic, lime juice, and coconut sugar (if using) for additional flavor. If you're using this sauce in the span of a few days, it will keep fine at room temperature, but it will last at least a few weeks in the refrigerator stored in an airtight jar.

Sugar

In Thailand, sugar will usually be in the form of white, refined sugar. However, I'd encourage you to use an unrefined form of sugar, many of which are now easily available in health food stores and conventional supermarkets. It also may be surprising to hear that sugar is a part of many Thai soups as a seasoning. Sugar has been rightfully vilified in recent years as the root cause of many health problems, such as type 2 diabetes and obesity. However, sometimes the demonization of foods goes to extremes. The decades-long demonization of fat and cholesterol is certainly a good example, as recent research has revealed that neither are the culprits in heart disease and in fact play essential roles in the functioning of our bodies. Contrary to popular belief in Western countries, sugar and other carbohydrates *can* have a place in our diet. Tropical countries like Thailand are a good example of this. And that is Thai Soup Secret #6.

Chiles in Vinegar
Prik Nam Som
Makes ½ cup

Nam som means *vinegar*. While my version calls for distilled white vinegar, you could use other types of vinegar, such as rice vinegar or even apple cider vinegar, though white vinegar is typically used in Thailand.

The chiles utilized here are on the milder side. While traditional Thai recipes call for a type of mild Thai chile that can be hard to find even in Asian supermarkets, jalapeños or serranos are perfectly good substitutes.

Ingredients

- 2 to 3 serranos or jalapeños
- ½ cup distilled white vinegar

Directions

Slice the serranos into approximately ¼-inch thick rings. In a medium jar with a tight-fitting lid, combine the serranos and vinegar. These will also keep well at room temperature in an airtight jar, but they will also last at least several weeks in the fridge.

CHAPTER 6
Thai Soup Secret #6: White Rice and Sugar Have Benefits

As a nutritional therapist that helps people with digestive issues, I mostly help people transition to low-carb diets. This means reducing or entirely removing sugar and grains, both of which can aggravate and disrupt proper gut function. This also means consuming liberal amounts of good-quality fat, protein, and, of course, bone broth, which will work wonders for an overwhelming majority of people with things like heartburn, GERD, IBS, chronic bloating, chronic constipation, and other intestinal issues. Many other connected issues (such as weight gain, blood sugar imbalances, hormonal imbalances, and even autoimmune issues) will often start to normalize as well.

Many other holistic practitioners and even conventional doctors and dietitians are now embracing low-carb diets. They've become so widely accepted in recent years that many people wrongly assume (and endlessly proselytize and argue on online forums) that all traditional diets everywhere are naturally low-carb.

Interestingly, anyone who has spent time in Thailand will tell you that Thai cuisine is anything but low-carb. The same could be said about every other Southeast Asian country. White rice is included with almost every meal, including soups. Ultra-sweet tropical fruit like pineapples and mangoes are available year-round. And sugar is used quite liberally to sweeten many dishes. The chronic health conditions that are often blamed on a high-carb diet in the West—such as type 2 diabetes, obesity, and heart disease—albeit becoming more common in Asia are still not nearly as widespread. Sometimes this is referred to as the "Asian paradox."

So, before we get to the recipes, I want to defuse some potential concerns as you'll see both white rice and sugar used throughout this cookbook. Let's start with white rice.

FIVE REASONS WHY WHITE RICE IS GOOD FOR YOU

1. White Rice Can Actually Help Stabilize Blood Sugar Levels

That may be odd to hear, as white rice is mostly starch and fairly high on the glycemic index. The glycemic index is commonly used to rank foods based on how they affect blood sugar. High-glycemic foods (such as sodas, fruit juices, sweetened breakfast cereals, candy, white bread, and, yes, white rice) can spike blood sugar levels more easily than other foods. Over time, high blood sugar can lead to weight gain and type 2 diabetes.

But there's something no one tells you about the glycemic index. It's a measurement of how a particular food affects blood sugar when that food is eaten *without other foods*.[19] Here's the key point: no one sits down to a meal of *only* white rice.

In Thailand, at least, white rice is always accompanied by other food—meats, vegetables, fats, and bone broth. This will slow down the body's digestive process, thus preventing blood sugar spikes that come from eating high-glycemic foods on their own.

Please understand, I'm not making a blanket statement that everyone should eat white rice. Certainly, type 2 diabetics and others with metabolic issues might do better with brown rice. But as someone who works with people with chronic digestive issues, I've noticed that white rice is particularly gentle on the digestive system.

2. White Rice Is Easy to Digest

Most people (including most doctors) don't know that whole grains can be hard for the body to digest if they're not *properly prepared*. The bran, the outer layer of all grains, including brown rice, contains something called phytic acid, which is an antinutrient that can cause digestive distress if not neutralized. Nature does this when a grain (which is essentially a seed) hits the earth and sprouts into a new plant. Moisture, warmth, and other soil conditions will naturally release the bran. Traditionally, cultures all around the world learned to mimic nature by soaking, sprouting, and fermenting grains. These proper preparations neutralize phytic acid (as well as other antinutrients in the bran) and make grains much more digestible.

Few people follow this protocol anymore because of the time involved, and few food companies do this for the same reason (time is money when you're a business). But this is not a problem with white rice as the bran has already been removed. People with chronic digestive issues will have a much easier time digesting white rice than brown rice.

3. White Rice Does Not Contain Gluten

White rice (as well as brown) is devoid of gluten and any of the other possibly problematic compounds that are a part of the three main sources of gluten (wheat, barley, and rye). No one knows exactly why gluten is causing so many health problems today. It could be that gluten itself is a complex and difficult protein for the body to digest. It could be that it's in so much junk food and that we eat so much of it. It could be the modern hybrids of wheat, which are thought to be higher in gluten than more historical strains. It could be the agricultural chemicals that are sprayed on wheat. Or it could be a combination of all those things. Whatever the reasons, it's a food that more and more people are becoming sensitive to. However, white rice is a very hypoallergenic food and presents none of those issues. It is a perfectly acceptable option if you're on a gluten-free diet.

4. White Rice Can Help With Chronic Digestive Issues

Many Eastern healing systems look at white rice as having certain qualities or energetic characteristics that can be beneficial beyond digestibility. For example, both Ayurveda, the ancient healing system of India, and Traditional Chinese medicine consider it a yin (or cooling) food that can help clear excessive heat and thus settle digestive upset in its many forms. Those from Asian countries know this well. Congee, a simple meal of white rice and bone broth, has countless variations throughout Asia and has been used for thousands of years for healing gut issues.

5. White Rice Is a Perfect Complement to Bone Broth

White rice combines beautifully with bone broth. Perhaps this is why so many Asian soups are served with either white rice on the side or directly in the soup as it easily absorbs and soaks up the flavor in broth. It also gives substance and heartiness to soups, which makes them much more satisfying, especially when consuming them as a full meal. And white rice's natural sweetness also complements other flavors in soups, especially spicy, salty, and sour flavors.

Speaking of natural sweetness, maybe it's time we reexamined our stance on sugar.

FIVE REASONS WHY IT'S OKAY TO ADD SUGAR TO YOUR SOUP

When I say "sugar," most people automatically think of white refined sugar. It's become so prevalent in the standard American diet (aptly abbreviated SAD) in the form of heavily processed foods, breakfast cereals, sweets, sodas, coffee drinks, commercial juices, candies, and baked goods that the average American now consumes around 150 pounds of refined sugar per year[20] and is completely unaware of it.

This unnatural and concentrated type of industrialized sugar can be harmful when consumed in large quantities (as most people in the West consume it). It's completely devoid of nutrients and can create dramatic swings in our body's normal blood sugar concentrations, which then creates a domino effect of problems. Short-term problems include fatigue, moodiness, digestive problems, and weight gain. Long-term problems include more chronic digestive issues, type 2 diabetes, heart disease, and obesity. I have little doubt that this high intake of refined sugar is the root cause of many Western diseases that are now becoming more common in Asian countries.

Unfortunately, you can't travel very far in Thailand these days without seeing refined sugar in many forms. Convenience stores stocking typical Western junk foods are ubiquitous. Soda is everywhere. Sweetened condensed milk is very popular. But before the global spread of industrialized junk food, it wasn't as if Thai people never ate sugar. They did. In fact, they even put sugar in soup. And so do many of the recipes in this book. That may sound strange until you realize *how* sugar is used in these recipes and the *type* of sugar that's used.

Specifically, I'm talking about *natural* sugars, which are vastly different than refined sugar. Let's briefly explore five reasons why natural sugars are okay to consume.

1. Natural Sugars Are Historical Foods

The popularity of low-carb diets like the Paleo Diet might make you think that before the advent of refined sugar, no one ate any sugar at all. But historically, almost every culture learned to take the natural sugars from its local environment and use them in its cuisine as sweeteners. Honey is the most obvious example. All around the globe, fruits have been dried to concentrate their sugars or pressed for their juices, which are then added to foods. Even sugarcane, the primary source of refined sugar today, has long been concentrated into a natural sweetener known as jaggery, which is still popular throughout the Eastern hemisphere.

Another very common worldwide source of natural sugar is the sweet sap that flows from trees. You probably know that in late winter and early spring throughout the northern United States and Canada, the sap from maple trees starts flowing. This sap is turned into maple syrup. This syrup-making process is very similar to the harvesting of sap that flows from the many different types of palm trees in Asia and Africa.

2. Palm Sugar Is the Historical Sugar of Thailand

Yes, palm sugar is the maple syrup of Thailand. And it is still used extensively throughout the country and exported throughout the world. You'll find it mostly in Asian supermarkets in two forms: a syrupy paste (though this form is not as viscous as maple syrup) or in hardened blocks (which can take different shapes). I prefer the paste form because it's a little easier to measure and dissolve in soups. It has a rich caramel flavor but isn't nearly as pronounced as, say, molasses.

3. Coconut Sugar Is a Type of Palm Sugar

Coconut sugar is a trendy natural sweetener that you'll now find in health food stores like Whole Foods and in well-stocked conventional supermarkets. What most people don't realize is that coconut trees are a type of palm tree; thus, coconut sugar is a type of palm sugar and will often be referred to as coconut palm sugar. It comes from the buds of coconut tree flowers (as opposed to the sap) and not the actual coconuts, so there's no coconut flavor to coconut sugar. It has a milder flavor than regular palm sugar and is sold in granulated form similar to refined sugar. It's also a sustainably produced natural sugar.[21]

4. Natural Sugars Were Historically Consumed in Moderation

In recent decades, there has been an increased awareness of the risks associated with a diet high in sugar. Many people are now going completely sugar-free with striking improvements to their health. I've seen this firsthand in myself and with many of my nutritional therapy clients. However, this doesn't mean all sugar is bad for us. Natural sugars actually contain a small number of nutrients, such as minerals, vitamins, enzymes, and fiber. But this doesn't mean one can simply substitute a large amount of natural sugar for an equally large amount of refined sugar. Natural sugars are still concentrated forms of sugar.

Jessica Prentice, in her book, *Full Moon Feast*, writes about the balance we need to maintain when it comes to natural sugar:

> How did traditional and indigenous diets use the sweet things they had, whether from sap, fruit, honey, or other source? Mainly they combined them with other elements of a meal. . . . The sweetness is woven into the larger meal, not a course of its own. This makes sense when you look at it from the point of view of health and wholeness. Sweetness, when it is accompanied by protein, fat, and vitamin-rich vegetables, and balanced by mineral-rich salt, soy sauce, fish sauce or broth, is absorbed by the body slowly, without the usual spike and crash.[22]

Beyond using natural sugar in moderation, there's another aspect that it will bring to the recipes in this book.

5. Natural Sugars Add Depth and Balance to Thai Soups

Natural sugars are not meant to make Thai soups sickeningly sweet. But that's really hard to do in soups anyway, because super sweet soups are just, well, kind of gross. Please add sugar slowly, to taste, in these recipes. It's meant to harmonize with other flavors (spiciness in particular, as sugar tempers the heat of chiles). It also adds contrasting notes to sour, bitter, and salty flavors.

When used in this way, natural sugars can be consumed the way they were meant to be consumed: in moderation, and, like white rice, in balance with other foods. This is the way all cultures used natural sugars before the advent of refined sugar.

Finally, although I recommend you use palm sugar or coconut palm sugar in these recipes, there are other natural sweeteners you can use, such as raw unrefined sugar and whole cane sugar. Please see my Thai soups resources page for some quality recommendations of natural sugars at www.fearlesseating.net/thai-soup-resources.

PART II
Recipes

Chapter 7
  Bone Broths: The Building Blocks of Thai Soups   45

Chapter 8
  Thai Drinking Broths: Simple Medicinal Recipes for Gut Health   59

Chapter 9
  Thai Congees: Restorative Rice Soups for Breakfast   69

Chapter 10
  Classic Thai Soups: Tom Yum, Tom Kha, and Beyond   83

Chapter 11
  Thai Fusion Soups: Fun and Creative Inspirations From Around the World   129

CHAPTER 7
Bone Broths: The Building Blocks of Thai Soups

Good broth resurrects the dead.
—South American proverb

You might think that I'm going to tell you that you really need to make a Thai-style bone broth for Thai soups. Actually, no. Though I'd encourage you to make a Thai-style broth, it's not a big deal if you choose to make bone broths in a more typical Western manner. Western-style broths are perfectly usable for all the recipes in this book, as the differences between them and Thai broths are fairly minor. Purists may disagree, but this book is intended for home cooks, and there's no sense in being a perfectionist about things when you're cooking for yourself or family and friends.

Thai broths—with their delicate notes of ingredients like lemongrass, ginger, or cilantro—will pair a little better with Thai soups, of course. And the short simmer time will make for a lighter broth, which also is more ideal for Thai soups than a heavier, richer broth. But a long-cooked Western broth will not ruin your soup. The beauty of broths is that they're so versatile for so many different types of soups. I'd encourage you to purposefully vary your broths each time you make them so you can start to taste how different ingredients add different notes of flavor.

Sometimes, though, making a broth just depends on what vegetable scraps you have hanging around. If that happens to be some carrots, onions, and celery, that's fine. Make a Western-style broth. And if you set out to make a light, clear broth but then get sucked into a long movie at home and totally forget about it (I've done this), only to find it's been boiling hours on end and is now cloudy and rich, well, it's still more than usable.

I'd also recommend making bone broths in large batches and storing them in the fridge and freezer. It's nice to have a few quarts of real broth on hand for making some quick, nutritious meals. If space is at a premium for you, consider investing in a small chest freezer. I have one that I use just for storing bones and broth.

On that note, let's start with the type of bone broth you're probably most familiar with and the type that your grandmother or great-grandmother made regularly.

Western-Style Bone Broth

Makes about 4 quarts

This bone broth is a basic but delicious recipe that boasts optional add-ins if you desire a gelatin-rich broth (see sidebar on following page).

Ingredients

- 3 to 5 pounds chicken, pork, or beef bones
- Water, as needed
- ¼ cup apple cider vinegar (for chicken and pork) or red wine (for beef)
- 2 to 3 medium carrots, cut into 1- to 2-inch pieces
- 2 to 3 ribs celery, cut into 1- to 2-inch pieces
- 1 medium to large onion, quartered
- 1 small bunch fresh parsley (optional)
- 1 small bunch fresh thyme (optional)
- 1 to 2 dried bay leaves
- 1 to 2 teaspoons whole black peppercorns

Directions

1. Place the bones in a large stockpot, cover them with water by about 1 to 2 inches, and add the vinegar. Let this mixture sit for 30 to 60 minutes.

2. Turn on the heat to high. Before the mixture boils, some foam, which is called "scum," will start to form on the surface. True to its name, it's not very pleasant looking, but it can't hurt you. Simply skim it off. You may not be able to get every last bit, but get as much as you can. Without skimming, the broth will become cloudier (which is not that big of a deal, but it may affect the visual appeal of the broth for some people). Different types of bones may produce more "scum" than others. Once you've skimmed the broth, add the carrots, celery, and onion.

3. Cover the stockpot, reduce the heat to low or medium-low, and bring the broth to a very gentle simmer. Add the parsley (if using), thyme (if using), bay leaves, and peppercorns.

For chicken or pork broth, simmer for 1 to 4 hours for a light broth; 4 to 8 hours for a moderately gelatinous broth; and up to 24 hours for a very gelatinous broth. For beef broth, simmer for 2 to 4 hours for a light broth; 4 to 8 hours for a moderately gelatinous broth; and up to 48 hours for a very gelatinous broth.

4. Let the broth cool for a few hours and strain out the solid ingredients. Transfer the broth to storage containers (see sidebar).

5. Store the broth in the fridge for up to 7 days and freeze whatever you won't use within 1 week. Broth will keep in the freezer for up to 3 months.

Tips and Variations

1. Though not necessary, you can roast the meaty bones first to develop more flavor. Put the bones in a roasting pan and roast them at 400°F for 30 to 40 minutes, or until the bones are browned on the outside but not charred. Add the roasted bones to the stockpot with the other, less meaty bones. This is more commonly done with pork or beef bones than with individual chicken bones. However, you can roast a whole chicken, remove the meat, and then use the carcass. You can also roast the veggies with the meaty bones too.

2. When the broth cools in the fridge, a layer of fat will form on the surface. Despite what every fat-phobic recipe on the Internet says, do not skim it off and throw it out. It will act as a seal and keep your broth fresher in the fridge for a longer period. When you do break the seal, you can use it as a cooking fat or feed it to your dog, who will love you for it!

Western-Style Bone Broth Add-Ins

Here are some optional gelatin-rich ingredients you can add to your Western-Style Bone Broth for heightened nutrition:

- Chicken backs, chicken feet, chicken giblets (necks, hearts, and gizzards)
- Pigs' feet (also called trotters)
- Oxtail, calf's foot

What Storage Containers Should You Use?

I recommend using wide-mouth glass mason jars for storage containers. If you're storing some of your broth in the freezer, keep in mind that liquids will expand in the freezer, so never fill your glass jar to the top or it will crack. Always leave an inch or two of space from the top of the jar.

I don't love using plastic storage containers because plastic can leach into food, but many people prefer plastic containers because they won't crack. If you're using plastic, try to use BPA-free containers and be sure the broth is thoroughly cooled before filling the containers.

3. Substitute turkey or duck carcasses in place of chicken. Substitute other types of red meat for beef (e.g., bison, venison, lamb, and so on).

4. For some of the longer cooking times, you may have to leave your stove on overnight. If you're uncomfortable doing this, simply turn it off before bed and leave the lid on the stockpot. The broth will still be warm in the morning. Bring the broth back to a boil and then return it to a gentle simmer.

Thai-Style Bone Broth

Makes about 4 quarts

A shorter simmer time and the use of Thai herbs and vegetables are the only major differences between a Thai-style broth and a Western one. But the result is a lighter broth with delicate hints of Thai herbs and veggies that is a better fit with Thai soups.

Ingredients

3 to 5 pounds chicken, pork, or beef bones

Water, as needed

1 to 2 stalks lemongrass, cut into 2- to 3-inch pieces (optional)

1 (1- to 2-inch) piece fresh galangal or ginger, peeled and coarsely chopped (optional)

4 to 5 cloves garlic (optional)

2 to 3 scallions, 1 small onion, or 2 to 3 small shallots (optional)

2 to 3 sprigs fresh cilantro, preferably with roots attached (optional)

1 teaspoon whole black or white peppercorns (optional)

2 to 3 ribs Chinese celery (optional; see sidebar on page 51)

Directions

1. Place the bones in a large stockpot and cover them with water by about 1 to 2 inches. Turn on the heat to high, and before the mixture boils, skim off any "scum" that rises to the surface. Cover the stockpot, reduce the heat to low or medium-low, and bring the broth to a very gentle simmer. If using, add the lemongrass, galangal, garlic, scallions, cilantro, peppercorns, and Chinese celery.

2. For chicken or pork broth, simmer for 1 to 4 hours. For beef broth, simmer for 2 to 4 hours.

3. Let the broth cool for a few hours and strain out the solid ingredients. Transfer the broth to storage containers (see sidebar on page 48). Store the broth in the fridge for up to 7 days and freeze whatever you won't use within 1 week. Broth will keep in the freezer for up to 3 months.

Tips and Variations

1. To make a really clear broth, you'll want to use mostly bones that are devoid of as much meat, fat, and blood as possible. In this case, avoid the more gelatinous parts (feet, backs, etc.), which may be hard to rid of all the excess grimy bits and pieces. Rinse the bones in water and then proceed with step 1 until you've skimmed off all the "scum." Don't add the other ingredients yet. Drain the water from the pot and start over with step 1 again, adding the other solid ingredients once the broth has come back to a simmer. This additional step of rinsing and skimming will make a clearer broth. You can do this with Western-style broths too if you'd like. Personally, I rarely do this as it adds more time to the process. I don't mind a slightly cloudy broth!

2. Beyond the vegetables listed in the ingredients, you can use almost any vegetable scraps. Cabbage, mushroom stalks, daikon radish, and traditional grocery-store variety celery are okay too.

Chinese Celery

Chinese celery has thinner stalks and a stronger flavor compared to Western celery. It's often found in Asian food markets. If you can't find it, Western celery is an acceptable substitute.

Plain Bone Broth

There is nothing wrong with making a bone broth without any vegetables, herbs, or spices. It may taste a little plain, but the point is, of course, to season it after the fact. Many Thai soups use the triple gem and pungent seasonings, such as fish sauce and chiles, that will turn any plain bone broth (or even water) into a wonderfully flavorful soup. The beauty of bone broth is that it is so very accepting of whatever you add. It will diffuse any and all seasonings equally, so that each spoonful is as tasty as the next.

To make a plain bone broth, simply use any type of animal bones and parts in any combination you want and follow the same process of skimming, simmering, straining, and storing as is outlined in the directions for the Western-Style Bone Broth (page 47) and the Thai-Style Bone Broth (page 50). Follow the simmer times for a light broth in the Thai style, or simmer longer if you want a more gelatin-rich broth in the Western style. The latter will take on a little more flavor from the longer simmer time, especially if you're using meatier bones.

Fish Broth

Makes 2 to 4 quarts (depending on size of fish carcasses)

Some of the recipes in this book use fish broth, which is, as far as I know, uncommon in Thailand. In fact, I never saw it used anywhere in any of my travels. Even more telling, I've never seen it used in any Thai recipe, either online or in a book (and that includes some of the more respected and well-known Thai chefs and cookbook authors). Perhaps this is because so many Thai soups use fish sauce, which in and of itself gives a subtle fish flavor. Or perhaps it's because so many seafood-based Thai soups include *whole* seafood—especially shrimp with the shells on and whole fish, which add more flavor (especially from the heads) than those that are shelled and filleted. Furthermore, seafood doesn't need a long simmer time to infuse a broth with a noticeable yet delicate taste of the sea.

Whatever the exact reasons fish broth is uncommon in Thailand, I've found that fish broth is still very adaptable with the soup recipes in this book that use seafood. It also happens to be the simplest bone broth to make, as it only requires a simmer time of, at most, one hour.

To make a fish broth, you'll need a good source of fish carcasses. Your local fishmonger will probably give them to you for practically nothing because so few people, at least in the United States, value them anymore. Any non-oily white fish (such as cod, snapper, and haddock) are fine to use. The delicate fats in oily fish such as salmon and tuna don't stand up well to heat and can yield an overly fishy broth. If you can get them, whole fish with the heads on are great to use as they contain valuable trace minerals and collagen.

Ingredients

1 to 2 cod, sole, haddock, or hake carcasses (or other non-oily fish carcasses), preferably with heads

Water, as needed

Directions

1. Place the carcasses in a stockpot and add enough water to cover the carcasses by 1 to 2 inches. (Please note that sizes of fish carcasses can vary widely. Larger carcasses will need a larger stockpot and vice versa.)

2. Turn on the heat to high, and before the water boils, skim off any "scum" that rises to the surface.

3. Reduce the heat to low or medium-low and bring the broth to a very gentle simmer. Continue simmering for about 1 hour.

4. Let the broth cool, strain out the solid ingredients, and store the broth in containers (see sidebar on page 48) in the fridge for 3 to 4 days. Freeze whatever you won't use within that time frame for up to 3 months.

How to Add More Flavor to Fish Broth

In Western circles, fish broth is often made with finely diced carrots, onions, and celery that are first sautéed in oil to bring out their flavors (because of the short simmer time), after which fish carcasses are added along with water. Everything is then simmered for 45–60 minutes.

But for the purposes of the recipes in this book, a plainer fish broth is best, as so many Thai seafood-based soups use herbs and seasonings that will add more than enough flavor on top of the fish broth. So, let's just keep this one simple—though if you want to add the vegetables and herbs from either the Western-Style Bone Broth (page 47) or Thai-Style Bone Broth (page 50), you certainly can.

Simple Shrimp Broth

Makes about 1 quart

Shrimp broth is interchangeable with fish broth and is actually the preferred option for some Thai soups, especially those that contain shrimp. While you could add the veggies and herbs from the Western-Style Bone Broth (page 47) or the Thai-Style Bone Broth (page 50), a simple base of shrimp shells, tails, and heads (if you can find them) is enough to make a nice, delicate broth that's great for Hot and Sour Soup with Shrimp (page 85) and other light seafood-based soups.

Ingredients

Shells, tails, and heads from 1 to 2 pounds shrimp

Water, as needed

Directions

1. Place the shrimp shells, tails, and heads in a small stockpot and add about 1 quart water (or enough to cover all the shrimp parts).
2. Bring the broth to a gentle simmer over medium heat. Simmer for 30 to 40 minutes.
3. Strain out the shrimp parts. If not using immediately, store in containers (see sidebar on page 48) in the fridge for 3 to 4 days. Freeze whatever you won't use within that time frame for up to 3 months.

Tips and Variations

1. To develop even more flavor, first sauté the shells, tails, and heads in 1 tablespoon olive oil or butter for 2 to 3 minutes, or until they start to turn pink. Shortly after they turn pink, they'll start browning slightly, at which point you'll add the water and follow the recipe directions in the same manner.
2. Shrimp heads can be sometimes hard to find, but they're worth the hunt—they're rich in fats, which will add additional flavor to the broth.

BONE BROTH FAQS

For something as simple as simmering bones in water, it's amazing how many questions I get. Let me address a few of the more common ones.

Where Do I Find Bones?

Always try to source the best-quality bones you can. That means bones from pastured and grass-fed animals, as animals on their natural diets will be more nutrient-rich and flavorful. The best options will be buying directly from local farmers and farmer's markets. Secondly, many health food stores and butchers are now selling good-quality bones due to the resurgence of interest in real bone broths. And, of course, save your bones! Keep any leftover bones from chicken, pork, beef, and seafood in a bag in your freezer until you have enough to make a broth.

What Are the Best Types of Bones to Use?

All types of bones will do. Generally speaking, a good mix of bones from different parts of the animal are best. Meaty bones give flavor, bones with marrow add nutrients, and bigger bones often result in a more gelatinous broth.

If you're looking to make a more gelatinous broth, then more gelatinous parts are good to find. For chickens, that means chicken feet, backs, and necks. For pork, a pig's foot is an excellent addition. And for beef, it's good to use the large, gelatinous knuckle bones, the oxtail, or even a calf's foot.

Can I Mix Bones from Different Animals?

Absolutely. I'll often throw chicken and pork together. Use whatever you have. It's all good!

Is It Best to Use a Whole, Raw Chicken or the Carcass from a Roasted Chicken?

Either one is fine. If you're using a whole, raw chicken, you can remove it from the stockpot after a few hours and take the meat from the bones. Just make sure the meat is tender and well cooked. Then return the carcass to the water and continue simmering.

Can I Use a Slow Cooker or a Pressure Cooker?

Yes. Personally, I prefer using a stockpot on the stove, as I find I can control the heat better (see the next question for more about temperature). Pressure cookers, especially the high-tech Instant Pot, have become very trendy in recent years, and they certainly save a lot of time. However, I find the flavor of broths cooked in these appliances somewhat flat.

For some of my recommended kitchen products (including good-quality stockpots, slow cookers, and things like strainers and storage containers), check out http://fearlesseating.net/fearless-broths-and-soups-resources.

At What Temperature Should I Simmer the Bones?

This depends on your desired outcome. If you want a more gelatinous broth from a longer cooking time, then that means a *very* gentle simmer, as boiling a broth for an extended period can damage the gelatin (though it won't ruin the broth). That means a barely perceptible simmer, usually at one of the lowest settings on your stove. A good indication of this kind of simmer is a few bubbles rising to the surface here and there.

For a short-cooked broth, a gentle rolling boil is fine.

Do I Need to Soak the Bones in Water First?

It's often recommended to first soak bones in water with an acidic medium, like apple cider vinegar, lemon juice, or wine. Acids will react with the minerals in bones and help break them down, giving you a broth richer in minerals. As far as I know, this is not a common practice in Thailand (perhaps due to the shorter simmering times). You don't have to soak bones before using them, but it certainly can't hurt.

How to Make Bone Broth 101

If you're really new to making broths and feel like you could use some basic how-to videos that walk you through it step-by-step, I have a very simple online course that teaches people how to make the five most basic bone broths: chicken broth, beef broth, pork broth, fish broth, and a mixed broth. You can find more info at www.howtomakebonebroth101.com.

CHAPTER 8
Thai Drinking Broths: Simple Medicinal Recipes for Gut Health

Dowager: When I was a girl—if I was ill—my mother's maid would make me the most delicious chicken broth.
Servant: There's nothing better than chicken broth as a pick-me-up.
Dowager: It really was delicious. I remember it to this day. She used to say, "Every good lady's maid should know how to make a restorative broth."

—Downton Abbey

Chances are you've never heard of a drinking broth. Essentially, a drinking broth (also called a sipping broth) is just broth flavored with different seasonings, and it's meant as a beverage, kind of like coffee. Truth be told, I'd never heard of drinking broths until recently, when a New York City chef opened a takeout window selling bone broth in to-go cups. I'm not joking. Google it.

The drinking-broth trend has caught on, and drinking broth is now offered in many places around the country (including health food stores, where you'll find various commercially boxed versions). Now, considering our ancestors didn't walk around drinking cups of broth, you might wonder if this is just another overhyped, ridiculous hipster food trend.

Well, I don't think so. Our ancestors didn't walk around drinking flavored iced coffee drinks or kale smoothies, but let's face it: those trends are not going away anytime soon. Times change, and I think there are some compelling cultural reasons why drinking bone broth may be around for a while.

Here's five to chew, er, sip on.

1. DRINKING BONE BROTH IS GREAT FOR YOUR GUT.

Chances are your ancestors didn't have IBS. Chances are they weren't taking acid blockers every day for chronic heartburn and GERD. Chances are they didn't have the two most common inflammatory bowel diseases for which there is no known cure, ulcerative colitis and Crohn's disease. Chances are they didn't have any of the increasingly common gastrointestinal disorders that now plague tens of millions of Americans. According to the National Institutes of Health, approximately one in five Americans now has some form of digestive disease.[23]

What is going on?

It would be foolish not to believe that the parallel rise of chronic disease and the industrialization of our food supply are not highly connected. Our ancestors would not recognize 90 percent of the "food" in supermarkets. Highly processed and loaded with pesticides, preservatives, GMOs, refined sugar, and unpronounceable ingredients, these items can wreak havoc with our gut lining.

An increasing number of people are seeking answers to their health problems in better-quality food. Considering millions are walking around with chronic gut issues, drinking bone broth in to-go cups is not such a crazy idea.

As we've seen in chapter 1 through chapter 3, a properly made bone broth is loaded with gut-healing nutrients that can help ease intestinal inflammation and repair a damaged gut lining.

2. DRINKING BONE BROTH IN THE MORNING IS MORE NOURISHING AND SUSTAINING THAN COFFEE.

As opposed to bone broth, coffee can actually *withdraw* nutrients from the body. This is due to the effect of caffeine, which is a diuretic and can cause the loss of vitamins and minerals as the body purges the caffeine. But caffeine also acts very much like sugar in the body, causing a temporary rise in blood glucose while stimulating the adrenal glands to release energy-boosting hormones and the central nervous system to release feel-good neurotransmitters, all of which give us a rush of energy and a mental lift.

While the effects of caffeine are nice, they are temporary and can lead to the opposite effect, which leaves us feeling lethargic and cranky. This usually ignites a craving for that second cup of coffee somewhere midmorning or perhaps midafternoon. For many people, this can lead to a dependence on caffeine and a nasty habit where we start consuming more than a moderate cup or two of coffee per day. Over the long haul, this can lead to further issues, like poor sleep, restlessness, irritability, sugar cravings, hypertension, and hormonal imbalances.[24]

To belabor the point, coffee is acidic and can exacerbate gastrointestinal issues such as heartburn, GERD, and gastritis. A study in 2014 showed that caffeine can inhibit collagen production in the skin.[25]

Try replacing that morning cup of coffee with bone broth instead. I know it sounds kind of strange. But trust me—it's so much healthier and can be a very helpful way to wean off or even entirely eliminate a serious caffeine dependence.

3. DRINKING BONE BROTH IN THE EVENING IS GREAT FOR A GOOD NIGHT'S SLEEP

So many of my clients tell me that sugar and junk food cravings peak at night, especially after dinner. When that urge hits, try warming up a cup of broth first. The mineral content of bone broth, especially calcium and magnesium, helps to calm and relax our muscles. These minerals also play important roles in regulating our sleep cycles.[26] The same goes for the amino acids in bone broth. A study by Japanese researchers found that glycine, one of the most abundant amino acids in bone broth, promotes alertness during the day and a restful night's sleep.[27]

If you have issues with insomnia, reducing caffeine and drinking bone broth can be a powerful one-two punch in resetting your body's natural cortisol rhythms. Basically, that means helping you relax and de-stress.

In my own life, I can attest to how much better I feel when I have either a good soup made with a homemade bone broth for dinner or a cup of broth after dinner. The urge to snack is reduced, and I feel so much calmer at night and sleep so much better.

4. DRINKING BONE BROTH IS GREAT FOR BUSY LIFESTYLES

Make a big pot of broth on the weekend that will last you all week and then transfer it to the fridge. Simply warm up a cup or two in the morning, season it to taste, put it in a travel coffee mug that will keep it hot, and you're good to go. A morning cup of broth takes as much time, if not less, as brewing a pot of coffee or even a cup of tea.

5. DRINKING BROTHS IS A GREAT WAY TO SAMPLE THE ESSENTIAL FLAVORS OF ETHNIC CUISINES

Because bone broth is such a welcoming medium, equally incorporating and diffusing whatever you add, it's a great way to taste and become familiar with the essential spices and herbs in different ethnic cuisines.

Thai food is a perfect example. Many common Thai dishes use quite a variety of herbs and spices that may be hard to identify as individuals. By using only a few ingredients in drinking broths, you'll become more familiar with their unique flavors.

In the Thai drinking broths that follow, I've attempted to incorporate all of the essential Thai ingredients into five simple recipes. This is a great place to start before we get to the actual soup recipes, as you will start to taste the subtle differences between, say, ginger versus galangal or Thai basil versus sweet basil. You'll also start to become familiar with the foundation of famous Thai soups, like tom yum and tom kha.

TO DISCARD THE TRIPLE GEM OR LEAVE IT IN?

It should be noted that when you're making recipes that contain the triple gem, you have the option of removing the lemongrass, galangal, and kaffir lime leaves or leaving them in the broth or soup before serving (the only exception to this would be the Thai-Style Bone Broth on page 50, in which case they're always removed). Remember, they're used as aromatics and not meant to be eaten. If you leave them in, you'll wind up having to eat around them, which can be both a little odd and annoying. On the other hand, fishing out individual pieces before serving the broth or soup can be a little tedious. To avoid this inconvenience, when simmering the aromatics in your soup or broth, you could tie them up in a mesh spice bag or a small piece of cheesecloth to contain them. However, I tried this once and felt things weren't as flavorful when the aromatics were not allowed to freely toss and tumble in the broth. Personally, I prefer to leave them in and don't mind sipping or spooning around them. This is how it's done in Thailand. When you leave them in, especially with a short simmer time, they'll continue to infuse your broth and soup with flavor. Furthermore, an occasional chomp on a fibrous piece of lemongrass or woody piece of galangal is no big deal. In fact, toward the end of my meal, when I can clearly identify the individual chunks of lemongrass and galangal, I'll spoon a few out and gently roll them in my mouth and suck out the remaining essence and flavor. I swear it's not as weird as it sounds.

Lemongrass, Galangal, and Kaffir Lime Drinking Broth

Makes 2 cups

This is basically the triple gem infused in broth with some Thai seasonings. It's the base of a tom yum soup but without the chiles and protein. So simple and yet so delicious.

Ingredients

2 cups bone broth (any variety; pages 47-54)

1 stalk lemongrass, cut into ¼-inch thick slices (page 23)

1 (1-inch) piece fresh galangal, peeled and cut into ⅛- to ¼-inch thick slices

3 to 4 kaffir lime leaves, ripped in half

4 to 6 fresh Thai basil leaves

1 to 2 teaspoons fish sauce, or to taste

Fresh lime juice, to taste

Directions

1. In a small pot over high heat, bring the broth, lemongrass, galangal, and kaffir lime leaves to a boil. Reduce the heat to medium-low or medium and simmer for 5 to 10 minutes.
2. Strain out the lemongrass, galangal, and kaffir lime leaves, if desired. Add the Thai basil leaves and season the broth with the fish sauce and lime juice.

Ginger, Lemongrass, and Mint Drinking Broth

Makes 2 cups

Imagine a minty medicinal herbal tea except with the added bonus of broth and a tongue-pleasing splash of salty and sour, and you'll come up with this exceptional broth.

Ingredients

- 2 cups chicken bone broth (pages 47-51)
- 1 (½- to 1-inch) piece fresh ginger, cut into ¼-inch thick slices
- 1 stalk lemongrass, cut into ¼-inch thick slices (page 23)
- 4 to 6 fresh mint leaves
- Salt or fish sauce, to taste
- Fresh lime or lemon juice, to taste

Directions

1. In a small pot over high heat, bring the broth, ginger, and lemongrass to a boil. Reduce the heat to medium-low or medium and simmer for 5 to 10 minutes.
2. Strain out the ginger and lemongrass, if desired. Add the mint leaves and season the broth with the salt and lime juice.

Sweet and Sour Drinking Broth

Makes 2 cups

This recipe is simple and straightforward—add some chiles if you desire a spicier version.

Ingredients

- 2 cups bone broth (any variety; pages 47-54)
- 2 to 3 cloves garlic, thinly sliced
- 1 to 2 fresh bird's eye chiles or pinch chile powder (optional)
- Small handful fresh cilantro leaves
- 1 to 2 teaspoons fish sauce
- Fresh lime juice, to taste
- 1 to 2 teaspoons coconut sugar

Directions

1. In a small pot over high heat, bring the broth and garlic to a boil. Reduce the heat to medium-low or medium and simmer for 4 to 5 minutes. If using fresh bird's eye chiles, add them with the broth and garlic. You can add the chiles whole for a mild kick of heat or slice them into ¼-inch thick rings for a spicier punch.

2. Add the cilantro leaves and season the broth with the fish sauce, lime juice, and coconut sugar.

Coconut Sweet and Sour Drinking Broth

Makes 2 cups

This is essentially the broth for the soup tom kha. It is very soothing—and very addictive. You may have to adjust the amount of broth if you desire a thinner or thicker consistency. For example, add a little less broth for a thicker consistency and vice versa.

Ingredients

1 (14-ounce) can full-fat coconut milk

½ cup chicken bone broth (pages 47-51)

1 stalk lemongrass, cut into ¼-inch thick slices (page 23)

1 (1-inch) piece fresh galangal, cut into ⅛- to ¼-inch thick slices

3 to 4 kaffir lime leaves, ripped in half

1 to 2 teaspoons fish sauce, or to taste

Fresh lime juice, to taste

1 to 3 bird's eye chiles, seeded and cut into ¼-inch thick slices (optional)

1 to 2 teaspoons palm sugar

Small handful fresh cilantro leaves

Directions

1. In a small pot over high heat, bring the coconut milk, broth, lemongrass, galangal, and kaffir lime leaves to a boil. Reduce the heat to medium-low or medium and simmer the broth for 5 to 10 minutes.
2. Season the broth with the fish sauce, lime juice, bird's eye chiles (if using), palm sugar, and cilantro.

Southern Thai Curry and Turmeric Drinking Broth

Makes 2 cups

With influences from Indonesia and Malaysia, southern Thai food is spicier than cuisine from other areas of Thailand. It incorporates a lot of dry spices that you might recognize from Indian cuisine. Curry powder (not a paste, but a blend of dry spices) and turmeric (widely known for its anti-inflammatory properties) give this broth an earthy flavor and a deep yellow-orange color.

Ingredients

2 cups bone broth (any variety; pages 47-54)

1 stalk lemongrass, cut into ¼-inch thick slices (page 23)

1 (1-inch) piece fresh galangal or ginger, cut into ⅛- to ¼-inch thick slices

1 teaspoon curry powder

½ teaspoon ground turmeric

Chile powder, to taste (optional)

Fresh lime juice, to taste

Fresh cilantro, to taste

Salt or fish sauce, to taste

Directions

1. In a small pot over high heat, bring the broth, lemongrass, and galangal to a boil. Reduce the heat to medium-low or medium, add the curry powder and turmeric, and simmer 5 to 10 minutes.
2. Season the broth with the chile powder (if using), lime juice, cilantro, and salt.

CHAPTER 9
Thai Congees: Restorative Rice Soups for Breakfast

It checks hunger, keeps off thirst, regulates wind, cleanses the bladder and digests raw remnants of food. Verily, monks, these are the five advantages of congee.

—The Buddha

Though not well-known in Western countries, congee is what I call "the oatmeal of Asia," where there are countless variations from China to Japan to India to Southeast Asia. Congee is basically a simple porridge-like soup of rice and broth that is typically eaten for breakfast. While rice and broth may sound boring, I promise you it is anything but. When combined with different types of meats, vegetables, herbs, and seasonings, you'll be amazed how something so simple can be so incredibly delicious.

Congee is also considered a very healing and restorative food, especially for those with weakened digestion and compromised immune systems, as it is light, easy to absorb, and soothing to the gut. It has been used medicinally for thousands of years in traditional Chinese medicine. In Bob Flaws's *The Book of Jook*—*jook* is the Chinese word for *congee*—there are over 250 restorative congee recipes geared toward different health conditions, including constipation, diarrhea, indigestion, stomach pain, and intestinal ulcers. If you suffer from acid reflux or any type of intestinal inflammation, a soothing bowl of congee in the morning will be so much better than the typical sugary American breakfast of highly processed boxed cereal, cold low-fat milk, and cold orange juice. Traditional Chinese medicine and other Eastern healing systems recommend a *warm* breakfast in the morning (especially in the colder months), as warm foods are closer to the body's internal temperature and are more easily digested.

In Thailand, congee is known as *jok* (pronounced like *joke*) and is so popular that even McDonald's has a version of it on their breakfast menu. Street vendors in Bangkok and beyond cater to busy working folks by selling jok to-go during the morning rush. Big simmering pots of rice in broth are simply spooned over pork meatballs or soft-boiled eggs and then seasoned with fish or soy sauce, sliced ginger, fried shallots, and fried garlic.

THE MAGIC OF FRIED SHALLOTS AND GARLIC

Although many Thai soups can be greatly enhanced by adding fried shallots and garlic, in my opinion, it's congee where these additions truly shine for a few reasons. First, Thai soups are renowned not just for their different flavors but also their different textures. And sometimes that includes the crunchy texture of things like bean sprouts, fresh herbs and veggies, and fried shallots and garlic. These are so popular in Thailand that they are sold commercially in stores. You'll probably see a few imported brands in Asian markets in the United States and other Western countries. However, there's nothing that can compare to freshly fried shallots and garlic, and that's the second reason they work so well. They add a vibrant, smoky flavor that contrasts beautifully with congee.

To make fried shallots and garlic at home, I use about 1 small shallot and 3 to 4 cloves garlic per bowl of congee. Finely chop the shallot and garlic. Melt 2 to 3 tablespoons coconut oil in a small wok over medium heat until the oil sizzles when you add a few drops of water. Add the shallot to the oil first and brown for about 1 minute and then add the garlic (which browns faster than the shallots) and cook for about 1 more minute. When fully submerged in the hot oil, the shallots and garlic will brown quickly and evenly in just a few minutes. If you sauté them in oil in a flat pan, it's much harder (and messier) to evenly brown them, though not impossible. Of course, you don't have to use shallots and garlic together. Many people prefer one or the other, but I love them both together.

Expertly frying shallots and garlic can take a little trial and error, depending on how thinly you slice the garlic, the type of pan you use, and the level of heat of your particular stove, but once you get it down, you'll find that perfectly fried shallots and garlic add a magical quality to congee and, of course, to many other soups.

HOW TO MAKE CONGEE

Congee is so simple to make. All you do is cook the rice at a very low simmer until the rice starts to lose its shape and break down. As the rice disintegrates, it will create a porridge-like consistency. You can use broth or water to cook the rice. For a small serving that you'll eat right away, use broth. However, I highly recommend making a large amount, in which case I'd suggest using water because a lot of liquid will evaporate while you simmer the congee. Personally, I hate losing all that broth! Making a large serving also means you won't have to spend an hour cooking congee every single time you make it. You can then store this in your fridge and warm up smaller portions with broth on the stove. Simply adding other ingredients and seasonings to these smaller portions will allow you to then make many different types of congee.

Just a few cups of rice will actually make a lot of congee. You want about 1 cup rice to about 6 to 10 cups water or broth. For a thinner, more soup-like consistency, use more liquid and vice versa. You can always add more liquid during the simmering if needed or cook the congee down more to thicken it.

In a large stockpot over high heat, bring the broth or water to a boil. Rinse the rice a few times under cool running water, and add it to the boiling liquid. Reduce the heat to the lowest setting on your stove and cook at a very low simmer with the pot's lid slightly ajar to let steam escape. Cook for 1 to 2 hours, until the rice grains break down, stirring frequently (this creates the porridge-like consistency of congee).

(I cannot overemphasize how important it is to stir frequently! Once the congee starts to thicken, it can easily burn on the bottom of the pot. And it can happen very quickly. Do *not* allow yourself to become easily distracted when making congee. A few minutes checking e-mail or Facebook can turn disastrous. I have spent more time than I wish to admit trying to scrape severely blackened rice off the bottom of my pots. Many of my pots still have visible rice burns.)

When the consistency of the rice is where you want it, remove the pot from the stove. Let it cool and then store it in the fridge, where the congee will thicken quite a bit from the starch in the rice. (Some say this creates a less than ideal flavor, but I've never noticed a big difference.) You'll now have a nice big pot of congee ready to go for the rest of the week. Simply add 1 to 2 cups congee with some broth, mixing the two together and creating the consistency you want. Bring the congee to a simmer in a small pot over medium heat and then add the other ingredients you're using (meats, eggs, veggies, and so on) and season it all to taste (the recipes below will give you a wide range of choices for seasonings). You've got yourself an awesome bowl of congee in the same amount of time it would take you to make a boring bowl of oatmeal.

What follows are seven simple Thai congee recipes. All of the serving sizes are for one person at 1 to 2 cups of previously cooked congee. If you're making the congee from uncooked rice, simply adjust the recipe directions by adding the other ingredients toward the end of the simmering time.

The beauty of congee is that it is so adaptable. Almost anything works. The thousands upon thousands of congee recipes around Asia are a testament to how versatile it can be. Experiment and find what you like!

Jok

Makes 1 serving

The first recipe is a fairly standard Thai jok that you'd find on the streets of Bangkok. Personally, I make this at home all the time and it is one of my absolute favorite breakfasts.

Ingredients

Pork Meatballs

¼ pound ground pork

1 to 2 cloves garlic, minced

1 to 2 teaspoons fish sauce or soy sauce

Congee

1 to 2 cups congee in pork or chicken bone broth (pages 47-51)

1 to 2 medium eggs

Seasonings, to Taste

Fresh ginger, sliced into matchsticks

Scallions, finely chopped

Fried garlic

Fried shallots

Fish sauce

Soy sauce

Freshly ground black or white pepper

Directions

1. In a medium bowl, mix the ground pork with the garlic and fish sauce. Form the mixture into bite-size meatballs.

2. Bring the congee to a simmer over medium or medium-high heat in a small pot. (Add more bone broth if needed to create a soupy consistency.) Add the pork meatballs and simmer for 2 to 3 minutes until the meatballs are fully cooked. (If you desire a thicker congee consistency, simmer the meatballs and eggs in broth separately and then add the congee.)

3. Add the eggs to the congee and poach them for about 2 minutes, or until the egg whites form and the yolks remain runny. Remove the congee from the heat (the eggs will continue to cook in the hot broth).

4. Ladle the jok into a serving bowl and season with the ginger, scallions, fried garlic, fried shallots, fish sauce, soy sauce, and pepper to taste. (Alternatively, you may use any combination of those to suit your own tastes.)

Thai Poached-Eggs Congee

Makes 1 serving

It doesn't get much easier than this recipe, which is particularly suited to those mornings when you're in a rush but still want to eat a nourishing, healthy breakfast. It takes all of about five minutes from start to finish.

Ingredients

- 1 to 2 cups congee in chicken or pork bone broth (pages 47-51)
- 1 to 3 medium eggs

Seasonings, to Taste

- Fish sauce
- Soy sauce
- Fresh chiles, thinly sliced, or chile powder
- Fresh ginger, sliced into matchsticks
- Fried garlic
- Fried shallots
- Fresh bean sprouts
- Fresh cilantro, coarsely chopped
- Fresh chives, coarsely chopped
- Fresh Thai basil leaves, coarsely chopped

Directions

1. Bring the congee to a simmer over medium or medium-high heat in a small pot. Add the eggs and poach them for 2 to 3 minutes, until the whites form and the yolks remain runny.
2. Ladle the congee into a serving bowl and season with the fish sauce, soy sauce, chiles, ginger, fried garlic, fried shallots, bean sprouts, cilantro, chives, and Thai basil to taste. (Alternatively, you may use any combination of those to suit your own tastes.)

Thai Chicken Congee

Makes 1 serving

Got some leftover chicken in the fridge? Sick of eating plain leftover chicken? This recipe will turn those boring leftovers into something that's anything but. This would make a great meal for lunch or dinner too!

Ingredients

- 1 to 2 cups congee in chicken bone broth (pages 47-51)
- 1 stalk lemongrass, cut into ¼-inch thick slices (page 23)
- 1 (1-inch) piece fresh galangal, cut into ⅛- to ¼-inch thick slices
- 3 to 4 kaffir lime leaves, ripped in half
- ½ cup cooked shredded chicken

Seasonings, to Taste

- Fish sauce
- Fresh chiles, thinly sliced, or chile powder (optional)
- Fried garlic
- Fried shallots
- Fresh cilantro, coarsely chopped

Directions

1. Bring the congee, lemongrass, galangal, and kaffir lime leaves to a simmer in a small pot over medium or medium-high heat. Simmer for 5 to 10 minutes.
2. Add the chicken to the congee and simmer for 2 to 3 minutes, until the mixture is heated through.
3. Ladle the congee into a serving bowl and season with the fish sauce, chiles (if using), fried garlic, fried shallots, and cilantro to taste. (Alternatively, you may use any combination of those to suit your own tastes.)

Pad Thai Congee

Makes 1 serving

Here's a simple take on Thailand's most famous stir-fried noodle dish, pad thai.

Ingredients

- 1 to 2 cups congee in pork or chicken bone broth (pages 47-51)
- 1 to 2 medium eggs
- 1 to 2 teaspoons palm sugar (optional)
- ¼ cup raw or roasted peanuts, or to taste
- 1 to 2 tablespoons fresh chives, coarsely or finely chopped
- ¼ to ½ cup fresh bean sprouts, or to taste

Seasonings, to Taste

- Fish sauce
- Chile powder
- Fried garlic
- 1 to 2 teaspoons palm sugar (optional)

Directions

1. Bring the congee to a simmer in a small pot over medium or medium-high heat. Add more broth if needed and add the eggs. Poach the eggs for 2 to 3 minutes, until the whites form and the yolks remain runny.
2. Add 1 teaspoon of the palm sugar (if using) and stir to combine thoroughly. Taste the congee and add the remaining 1 teaspoon palm sugar, if desired.
3. Add the peanuts and chives to the congee and then top it with the bean sprouts.
4. Ladle the congee into a serving bowl and season with the fish sauce, chile powder, fried garlic, and palm sugar (if using) to taste. (Alternatively, you may use any combination of those to suit your own tastes.)

Thai-Chinese Duck and Pickled Veggie Congee

Makes 1 serving

You might find a recipe like this in Bangkok's Chinatown more so than other parts of Thailand. While duck is used extensively throughout Thai cuisine, it's more commonly included in congees in Chinese cuisine. You can find duck in most Asian food stores and in some health food stores too. Its meat is similar to chicken, but more tender and juicy due to the higher fat content. Duck eggs, slightly larger with a harder shell than chicken eggs, are now commonly sold at Whole Foods and farmer's markets. Pickled veggies complement congees well, adding a sour component and a crunchy texture. If pickled mustard greens sound a little too weird, try adding a dill pickle, chopped into bite-size pieces. It works!

Ingredients

- 1 to 2 cups congee in chicken or pork bone broth (pages 47-51)
- 1 to 2 medium duck eggs
- ½ cup cooked shredded duck
- ¼ to ½ cup pickled mustard greens or other pickled vegetables

Seasonings, to Taste

- Fish sauce, soy sauce, or oyster sauce
- Chile powder
- Fried garlic
- Fresh Thai basil leaves, coarsely chopped

Directions

1. Bring the congee to a simmer in a small pot over medium or medium-high heat. Add the duck eggs and poach them for 2 to 3 minutes, until the whites form and the yolks remain runny.
2. Add the duck and simmer 1 more minute.
3. Add the mustard greens, stirring to combine.
4. Ladle the congee into a serving bowl and season with the fish sauce, chile powder, fried garlic, and Thai basil to taste. (Alternatively, you may use any combination of those to suit your own tastes.)

Thai Shrimp Congee

Makes 1 serving

Congee is so incredibly versatile, so why not shrimp? You could easily use any type of seafood you want in place of shrimp: fish, crab, lobster, squid, and so on. Congee works with just about anything.

Ingredients

- 1 to 2 cups congee in fish or shrimp broth (pages 52-54)
- 1 stalk lemongrass, cut into ¼-inch thick slices (page 23)
- 1 (1-inch) piece fresh galangal, cut into ⅛- to ¼-inch thick slices
- 3 to 4 kaffir lime leaves, ripped in half
- ½ cup whole, peeled shrimp

Seasonings, to Taste

- Fish sauce
- Fresh chiles, thinly sliced, or chile powder
- Fried garlic
- Fried shallots
- Scallions, finely chopped
- Fresh cilantro, coarsely chopped

Directions

1. Simmer the congee, lemongrass, galangal, and kaffir lime leaves in a small pot over medium or medium-high heat for 5 to 10 minutes.
2. Add the shrimp and simmer 2 to 3 minutes, until the shrimp turn pink and are cooked through.

3. Ladle the congee into a serving bowl and season with the fish sauce, chiles, fried garlic, fried shallots, scallions, and cilantro to taste. (Alternatively, you may use any combination of those to suit your own tastes.)

Sweet Coconut-Mango Congee

Makes 1 serving

I know savory breakfasts are not the norm in America, so here's one if you're not quite ready to give up your sweet tooth. This is deceptively addictive, so be careful not to overdo it. It has a lot in common with Thailand's most popular dessert, mango sticky rice, and you could easily chill this in the fridge and serve it as a sweet treat. It would surely be a lot healthier than what most people eat for dessert these days.

Ingredients

- 1 cup congee in water
- ½ cup coconut milk or coconut cream
- 1 to 3 teaspoons palm sugar
- 1 mango, peeled and chopped into about 1-inch chunks
- Fresh lime juice (optional)

Directions

1. Bring the congee and coconut milk to a simmer in a small pot over medium or medium-high heat.
2. Transfer ¼ to ½ cup congee to a small bowl. Dissolve 1 teaspoon of the palm sugar into the congee. Return the sweetened congee to the pot and stir well. Taste the congee and add the remaining 1 to 2 teaspoons palm sugar, if desired.
3. Remove the congee from the heat and top with the fresh mango. Season the congee to taste with the lime juice (if using).

CHAPTER 10

Classic Thai Soups: Tom Yum, Tom Kha, and Beyond

Soup is a lot like family. Each ingredient enhances the others; each batch has its own characteristics; and it needs time to simmer to reach full flavor.

—Marge Kennedy

In this chapter are fourteen classic Thai soup recipes that you will find in various incarnations throughout Thailand. Even if you've never been to Thailand, you will probably recognize the first two recipes: tom yum and tom kha, the iconic soups of Thai cuisine.

The rest of the recipes are not as easy to find outside Thailand. While you may find them on some international Thai menus, they haven't become as standardized as tom yum and tom kha. They often have dramatically different tastes and ingredients, depending on which region of Thailand they come from. For example, you'll often find a small selection of noodle soups on international Thai menus, but Thai noodle soups are so diverse with so many influences that it's almost impossible to find two noodle soups that are the same. I consider that a good thing.

Sometimes it's good to make recipes without any preconceived idea of how they should taste! Without the expectation of how you think it should be, you're less likely to be disappointed and think the results are not authentic. But don't get too hung up on making things authentic. Over time, influences from near and far have shaped and changed Thailand's cuisine, introducing new foods and flavors. This happens everywhere and is one of the reasons I think the word *authentic*—when describing any cuisine—can be a little misleading. For example, did you know that bird's eye chiles (and other chile varieties grown in Thailand) are not native to Thailand? They were actually introduced by Portuguese traders in the sixteenth century. Food customs change and evolve too. Traditionally, soup in Thailand was more of a side dish that would accompany the main meal. While this is still true today, many soups are now full meals on their own, part of busy street-food culture for working folks needing a quick meal. What's considered authentic today probably wasn't considered authentic a hundred years ago, and at the current pace of globalization, it surely won't be considered authentic a hundred years from now.

My point is to allow these recipes to guide you; however, don't feel you have to follow them too literally. Remember Thai Soup Secret #5 (page 31)! You'll learn a lot from making each soup differently every time, altering a few things, changing up the veggies or the meats, and, of course, adjusting the seasonings.

Hot and Sour Soup with Shrimp

Tom Yum Goong

Makes 3 to 4 servings

Thailand's most famous soup, tom yum is the king of all Thai soups. Popular throughout Thailand, it's on every menu in every Thai restaurant outside of Thailand too, and rightfully so. All the quintessential flavors of Thailand are present here, and though variations are widespread, there are three essential elements: The first is the fragrant triple gem of lemongrass, galangal, and kaffir lime infused in broth. The second is the heat of bird's eye chiles. And the third is seasoning it all to taste with the sour and salty flavors of lime juice and fish sauce.

After those three constants, you'll see tons of differences among recipes for this soup. Shrimp (*goong* means *shrimp*) is the most common protein, though other types of seafood and even chicken can be used too. Some versions use sugar to give it a little added sweetness. Some use different vegetables. Many versions add coconut milk or even cow's milk to give it a creamy consistency. Many also use a canned tom yum paste that's simply dissolved in the broth, though I would encourage you not to take this shortcut as this just can't compare to fresh ingredients! Also, most commercial tom yum pastes use MSG, soybean oil (a very poor-quality oil), and other chemical flavorings.

> **Chiles, Chiles, Chiles!**
>
> Depending on your personal love or hate of heat and spice, you can use as many or as few chiles as you want. Many recipes call for using a lot more than what I've included here, though I've found even just three bird's eye chiles add an intense punch of heat. Start with one chile, taste the soup, and add more if needed. Or leave them out entirely if you want. It won't exactly be traditional without chiles, but who the heck cares. Ask a hundred native Thais what's the most traditional version of tom yum, and you'll get a hundred different answers. All that matters is what you like. Even without chiles, it will still have plenty of flavor.

Ingredients

- 1 quart fish broth, shrimp broth, chicken bone broth (pages 47-54), or water
- 2 stalks lemongrass, cut into ¼-inch thick slices (page 23)
- 1 (1-inch) piece fresh galangal, cut into ⅛- to ¼-inch thick slices
- 8 to 10 kaffir lime leaves, ripped in half
- 1 to 3 bird's eye chiles, sliced into thin rings (see sidebar)
- 1 medium onion, coarsely chopped
- 1 medium tomato, coarsely chopped
- 1 cup oyster, shiitake, or straw mushrooms, wiped clean and coarsely chopped
- ¼ to ½ cup fish sauce, or to taste
- ¼ to ½ cup fresh lime juice, or to taste
- 15 to 20 large shrimp, cleaned and peeled or left whole
- Cooked jasmine rice, for serving (optional)

Seasonings, to Taste

Fish sauce

Coconut sugar

Scallions, finely chopped

Fresh cilantro, coarsely chopped

Lime wedges

Directions

1. Bring the broth to a gentle boil in a medium to large pot over medium-high or high heat. Reduce the heat to medium-low or medium and add the lemongrass, galangal, and kaffir lime leaves and simmer about 10 minutes.
2. Add the bird's eye chiles, onion, tomato, and mushrooms, and simmer for 4 to 5 minutes.
3. Add ¼ cup of the fish sauce and ¼ cup of the lime juice, slowly adding more of each, up to ½ cup (or more, to taste).
4. Add the shrimp and simmer for 2 to 3 more minutes, until the shrimp turn pink and are cooked through.
5. Ladle the soup into individual bowls and season with the fish sauce, coconut sugar, scallions, and cilantro to taste. Serve with lime wedges on the side. (Alternatively, you may use any combination of those to suit your own tastes.)
6. For a more complete meal, serve the soup with jasmine rice on the side (if using).

Coconut Chicken Galangal Soup

Tom Kha Gai

Makes 1 to 2 servings

If tom yum goong is the king of Thai soups, tom kha gai is the queen. Some might even say it's superior to tom yum in popularity. Whichever rules supreme, I can't say for sure, but both are equally featured on Thai menus all over the world. And both have many similarities. They both use the triple gem of lemongrass, galangal (*kha* means *galangal*), and kaffir lime leaves. They both use bird's eye chiles. They both use similar seasonings. And they both feature different types of meats, though chicken (*gai* means *chicken*) is probably most commonly used in tom kha. The main difference is that tom kha always uses coconut milk.

My version of tom kha gai is inspired from the island of Ko Lanta in southern Thailand. The Thai family that ran the guesthouse where I stayed made the absolute best version of the soup I had anywhere in Thailand. One day, I asked if I could come into the kitchen to observe how they made it. I wanted to document how they made it so I could re-create it in America. They were surprised that a foreigner was so interested in their cuisine, and they welcomed me with open arms. I'll never forget the smiles on their faces as I stood there taking notes and snapping pictures.

> **How Many Chiles Should You Use?**
>
> For a mild spice, use only one chile; for a medium spiciness, use two; and for a really good kick, use three or more. For zero kick, don't use any chiles at all.

Ingredients

- 1 to 2 cups chicken bone broth (pages 47-51)
- 1 (14-ounce) can full-fat coconut milk
- 2 stalks lemongrass, cut into ¼-inch thick slices (page 23)
- 1 (1-inch) piece fresh galangal, cut into ⅛- to ¼-inch thick slices
- 8 to 10 kaffir lime leaves, ripped in half
- 2 to 3 cooked or raw chicken thighs or breasts, cut into 1-inch pieces
- 1 to 3 bird's eye chiles, sliced into thin rings (see sidebar)
- 1 medium onion, coarsely chopped
- 1 medium tomato, coarsely chopped
- 1 cup oyster, shiitake, or straw mushrooms, wiped clean and coarsely chopped
- Cooked jasmine rice, for serving (optional)

Seasonings, to Taste

- Fish sauce
- Fresh lime juice
- Coconut sugar
- Fresh cilantro, coarsely chopped
- Scallions, finely chopped

Directions

1. Bring the broth and coconut milk to a gentle boil in a medium pot over medium-high or high heat. (For a thicker consistency, use less broth and more coconut milk and vice versa.)

2. Add the lemongrass, galangal, and kaffir lime leaves and reduce the heat to medium-low or medium and simmer 5 to 10 minutes.

3. Add the chicken. For cooked chicken, gently simmer for 1 minute to reheat. For raw chicken, simmer for 2 to 3 minutes or until it's cooked through and no longer pink in the middle. Be sure not to boil the soup, as this will make the chicken overly tough.

4. Add the bird's eye chiles, onion, tomato, and mushrooms and simmer for 2 to 3 more minutes.

5. Ladle the soup into individual bowls and season with the fish sauce, lime juice, coconut sugar, cilantro, and scallions to taste. (Alternatively, you may use any combination of those to suit your own tastes.)

6. Serve with a side of jasmine rice (if using).

Chicken and Rice Soup

Khao Tom Gai

Makes 3 to 4 servings

Don't let the chiles in the picture fool you. They're optional and, more often than not, this is a very plain soup served without chiles. It's frequently served for breakfast in Thailand but can be had at other times of the day too. And though it resembles a congee, the rice here is not cooked into a porridge.

This is one of my go-to recipes when I come home and don't have anything planned for dinner. Within twenty minutes, I can have this ready. Beyond its simplicity, there are a few other reasons I love this recipe. The first is the lemongrass- and galangal-infused broth. Next is that you can make this as basic or complex as you want. If you're battling a cold or digestive issue, make it more broth-based and keep the seasonings to a minimum. If you want something heartier, add more chicken and rice and go crazy with the seasonings. In particular, fried shallots and garlic are my favorite additions, as they add that wonderful crunch and smoky flavor that can make any plain soup really come alive.

Ingredients

1 quart chicken bone broth (pages 47-51)

1 cup uncooked jasmine rice

1 stalk lemongrass, cut into ¼-inch thick slices (page 23)

1 (1-inch) piece fresh galangal, cut into ⅛- to ¼-inch thick slices

1 cup cubed cooked or raw chicken pieces

Seasonings, to Taste

Fish sauce

Fresh chiles, thinly sliced

Chile powder

Fried shallots

Fried garlic

Scallions, finely chopped

Fresh cilantro, coarsely chopped

Directions

1. Bring the broth, rice, lemongrass, and galangal to a gentle boil in a medium to large pot over high heat. Reduce the heat to medium-low or medium and simmer, covered, until the rice is cooked, about 10 minutes. Add the raw chicken, if using, and simmer until it is cooked through and no longer pink in the middle, about 2 to 3 minutes. If you are using cooked chicken, add it at the last minute and simmer until it is warmed through.

2. Ladle the soup into individual bowls and season with the fish sauce, chiles, chile powder, fried shallots, fried garlic, scallions, and cilantro to taste. (Alternatively, you may use any combination of those to suit your own tastes.)

Vegetable Soup

Gaeng Jued

Makes 3 to 4 servings

Here's a super simple recipe that's frequently given to those that are sick. *Gaeng jued* means *plain soup* or *bland soup* in Thai, but that doesn't mean it doesn't taste good. Light broths with only a handful of herbs and seasonings can be just as flavorful as more complex soups with many ingredients. For example, curries can contain well over a dozen different types of herbs, spices, and roots, which all blend wonderfully. But you'd be hard-pressed to identify the lemongrass or any other ingredient. With gaeng jued and other broth-based soups, you can identify specific flavors and learn to really appreciate their fragrance and flavor.

You can also make this soup quite hearty with the addition of jasmine rice and pork meatballs. In Thailand, pork meatballs are frequently included. That may seem a little odd for what's considered a light and plain meal (and a vegetable soup), but meat is viewed as extremely healthy in Thailand, including pork. Nor is this soup—or any Thai soup, for that matter—overloaded with meat. Most soups have small amounts of meat that act in balance with the other elements of the soup. Because bone broth is a good source of amino acids, it's considered to have what's called a protein-sparing effect. This means it reduces the body's need for protein. Perhaps this is why so many Asian soups contain small to moderate amounts of meat. You could certainly leave out the meatballs if you want. Many versions of this soup use tofu in place of pork (and many include both).

> **Try Some Asian Vegetables**
>
> If you're hankering to mix up the vegetables in this soup, you can experiment with some Asian veggies if you have an Asian market nearby. Different types of bamboo shoots, radishes, mushrooms, gourds, root vegetables, greens, and celery are frequently found in the produce section of Asian markets and would all be perfectly fine to use.

Ingredients

Pork Meatballs

- ½ pound ground pork
- 1 to 2 cloves garlic, minced
- 2 teaspoons oyster sauce
- 1 tablespoon fish sauce or soy sauce

Soup

- 1 quart chicken or pork bone broth (pages 47-51)
- 2 to 3 cups coarsely chopped vegetables of your choice (e.g., greens, Chinese cabbage, carrots, and mushrooms)
- Cooked jasmine rice, for serving (optional)

Seasonings, to Taste

Fish sauce

Chile powder

Fried garlic

Scallions, finely chopped

Fresh cilantro, coarsely chopped

Directions

1. In a medium bowl, mix together the ground pork, garlic, oyster sauce, and fish sauce. Form the mixture into bite-size meatballs and set them aside.

2. Bring the broth to a gentle boil in a medium pot over medium-high or high heat. Add the meatballs and vegetables, reduce the heat to medium-low or medium, and simmer about 5 minutes. (Add softer veggies like greens and cabbage toward the end of the cooking time, so as not to overcook them.)

3. Ladle the soup into individual bowls and season with the fish sauce, chile powder, fried garlic, scallions, and cilantro to taste. (Alternatively, you may use any combination of those to suit your own tastes.)

4. Serve with a side of jasmine rice (if using).

Sweet and Sour Pineapple Soup with Pork

Tom Jued Samparod Se Krong Moo

Makes 3 to 4 servings

I'll never forget the first meal I had in Bangkok's Chinatown the morning after I'd arrived from America. If you've ever traveled to Thailand from America, you know that international flights arrive around midnight. I'd barely slept, felt like death, and was wide awake before 6 a.m. I crawled out of bed and headed down the street to find only one place open. I ordered a simple pork and winter melon soup. After a few sips, it was like someone had hooked me up to an IV and reinvigorated my whole body. I could feel the energy slowly soak back in. It was exactly what I needed at that moment, and I'll never forget how good it felt.

This recipe resembles that one, but instead of winter melon, which may not be easy to find even in Asian markets, it uses pineapple, a common addition to soups and curries in Thailand. You'll find many Chinese-influenced soups like this in Thailand that are essentially just a flavorful broth, one type of meat, and one type of fruit or vegetable. It seems so plain, but there's just something about a salty broth and a sweet piece of fruit together that is so nourishing and restorative.

For this recipe, I use pork belly as an alternative to more common cuts of pork, which will give the soup a rich, smoky flavor. Feel free to use any other cut of pork instead.

Ingredients

1 teaspoon whole white peppercorns

1 clove garlic

1 quart water or pork bone broth (pages 47-51)

½ pound pork belly, cut into small cubes

Half of a whole pineapple, peeled and chopped into small cubes (about 2 cups)

1 tablespoon palm sugar

1 tablespoon fish sauce

1 small bunch watercress or spinach (about 2 to 3 tightly packed cups), stems removed

Seasonings, to Taste

Fish sauce or soy sauce

Chile powder

Coconut sugar

Freshly ground white or black pepper

Fresh cilantro, coarsely chopped

Directions

1. Pound the peppercorns and garlic with a mortar and pestle into a paste (alternatively, you can use a food processor). Set the paste aside.

2. Bring the water to a gentle boil in a medium pot over high heat. Add the peppercorn paste, pork belly, pineapple, palm sugar, and fish sauce. Return to a boil and reduce the heat to low or medium-low. Simmer, covered, for about 30 minutes.

3. Skim off any fat or "scum" that rises to the surface, add the watercress, and simmer for 1 or 2 minutes longer, until the greens gently wilt.

4. Ladle the soup into individual bowls and season with the fish sauce, chile powder, coconut sugar, pepper, and cilantro to taste. (Alternatively, you may use any combination of those to suit your own tastes.)

Southern Thai Hot and Sour Curry Soup

Gaeng Som

Makes 3 to 4 servings

When I first saw orange curry on a menu in southern Thailand, I was a bit confused. I was aware of yellow, red, and green curries, but I'd never heard of orange. Always up for new culinary adventures, I ordered it out of curiosity. The server asked me how spicy I wanted it. In Thailand, Westerners are usually given a few options: a little spicy, moderately spicy, and "Thai spicy."

Thai spicy means *very spicy*—in theory, anyway. Because very few Westerners ask for things Thai spicy, sometimes they err on the side of caution and tone it down. But not always.

This was one of those occasions where Thai spicy really meant light-your-mouth-on-fire Thai spicy. At the end of my meal, I'd used so many napkins to wipe my watering eyes and running nose that my table looked like it was in the path of a ticker tape parade. I was sucking air for a good fifteen minutes after the meal just to cool my mouth down. But I still loved every sip of the orange curry and had it many more times in my travels (though I never again ordered it Thai spicy).

I learned later on that orange curry is another name for the classic southern Thai hot and sour curry soup. The orange color comes from turmeric, though it's often more of a reddish-orange color from the curry paste. And the curry paste in the south of Thailand is fiery hot, partly due to the chile paste itself and partly due to the fact that there's no coconut milk in this soup, which tempers the heat of curry pastes. (For more information on how to customize this recipe to your own spice and flavor preferences, see the sidebar on page 53.)

Ingredients

Gaeng Som Curry Paste

30 to 40 dried bird's eye chiles or chiles de árbol or 8 to 10 large dried California chiles

3 to 4 cups boiling water

1 to 2 small shallots

1 to 2 cloves garlic (optional)

1 (1-inch) piece fresh turmeric, coarsely chopped

1 to 2 teaspoons shrimp paste

Soup

1 quart fish broth, shrimp broth (pages 52-54), or water

1 to 4 tablespoons Gaeng Som Curry Paste (page 100)

2 to 4 tablespoons fresh lime juice

2 cups coarsely chopped vegetables of your choice (e.g., Chinese cabbage, green beans, and daikon radish)

1 (½-pound) fish fillet of your choice (snapper, cod, grouper, etc.) or ½ pound shrimp (or a combination of fish and shrimp)

Cooked jasmine rice, for serving (optional)

Seasonings, to Taste

Fish sauce or salt

Coconut sugar

Fresh lime juice

Directions

1. Place the chiles in a large heat-resistant bowl. Pour the boiling water over the chiles and let them soak until they soften, about 20 to 30 minutes.

2. Add about ¼ cup of the soaking water and about 30 of the bird's eye chiles or all of the California chiles (no need to be cautious with these chiles, as they're so mild), 1 of the shallots, 1 of the cloves garlic (if using), half of the turmeric, and 1 teaspoon of the shrimp paste to a blender and blend until a paste is formed.

3. Taste the curry paste and add the remaining 10 bird's eye chiles, shallot, clove garlic, turmeric, and 1 teaspoon shrimp paste if desired. Transfer any leftover chile paste to a lidded glass jar and store in the fridge for up to 1 week.

4. Bring the broth to a simmer in a medium pot over medium-high heat. Add 1 tablespoon of the Gaeng Som Curry Paste and 2 tablespoons of the lime juice. Stir to combine and taste the broth. Continue adding more curry paste and lime juice, 1 tablespoon at a time, to your preferred taste.

5. Add the vegetables and simmer for 3 to 5 minutes, until they are tender but not overcooked.

6. Add the fish or shrimp and simmer for 2 to 3 minutes, until cooked through.

7. Ladle the soup into individual bowls and season with the fish sauce, coconut sugar, and lime juice to taste. (Alternatively, you may use any combination of those to suit your own tastes.)

8. Serve with a side of jasmine rice (if using).

A Simple Curry Paste

This recipe is one of only two recipes in this book that uses curry paste—because it's so simple. Unlike the traditional red, green, and yellow curry pastes (which are very time- and ingredient-intensive), this orange one is not. It only requires a handful of things and can be whipped up very quickly.

It should also be noted that this is the only recipe in the book that uses shrimp paste, a highly pungent but very flavorful paste that's common in Thai cuisine. You'll find shrimp paste in Asian markets. Shrimp paste is similar to fish sauce in that it adds a salty, umami flavor to dishes. It's also similar in that the smell can be off-putting (but the taste isn't nearly as intense). So, don't freak out when you first open it. Of course, if you live with people who may not be used to the smell of shrimp paste, prepare for some comments along the lines of, "What the #%#& is that smell?" I speak from experience here. You will be harshly judged. Just a heads-up.

Because the curry paste is so intense and flavorful, this soup recipe typically uses water instead of broth as a base. If you can't find shrimp paste (or don't want to use it), then use a fish or shrimp broth.

You can also choose the type of chile you want to use in the curry paste. For a spicy version, use dried bird's eye chiles or chiles de árbol. For a much milder version, use dried California chiles. All of these are found in most Asian supermarkets. If you can't find them locally, they can be easily ordered online.

I have to be honest, though: I don't love this soup without any heat. It's not really a southern-Thailand version without it. That being said, there are countless incarnations of this soup throughout Thailand, many of which are only mildly spicy. If you are brave enough to try the spicy version, be sure to serve it with a side of jasmine rice, which will help reduce the intensity a bit.

Northeastern Herbal Curry Soup

Gaeng Om

Makes 3 to 4 servings

Similar to the Southern Thai Hot and Sour Curry Soup (page 99), this is a broth-based soup using a simple curry paste that is not a typical Thai curry paste with lots of ingredients. The paste is dissolved in broth, and the broth is then loaded with veggies and herbs. This creates a very fragrant, light, and complex soup bursting with flavor. Chicken works well here, but you could easily use other types of meats and seafood as well as different veggies and herbs.

Ingredients

Curry Paste

2 stalks lemongrass, cut into thin slices

1 (1- to 2-inch) piece fresh galangal, cut into thin slices

2 to 4 bird's eye chiles, seeded

3 to 4 small shallots, coarsely chopped

3 to 4 cloves garlic, coarsely chopped

Soup

1 quart chicken bone broth (pages 47-51)

1 tablespoon fish sauce

4 to 5 kaffir lime leaves, ripped in half

1 cup shredded cooked or raw chicken

1 cup cubed butternut squash

1 cup mushrooms (any variety), coarsely chopped

1 cup fresh green beans, trimmed and cut into 1-inch pieces

1 cup shredded Chinese cabbage

3 to 4 scallions, thinly sliced

1 bunch fresh dill (about 1 loosely packed cup), stems included, cut into 1-inch strips

½ cup loosely packed fresh Thai basil leaves

Cooked jasmine rice, for serving (optional)

Seasonings, to Taste

Fish sauce

Fresh Thai basil leaves, coarsely chopped

Scallions, finely chopped

Fresh lime juice

Directions

1. Using a mortar and pestle or a food processor, pound or blend the lemongrass, galangal, bird's eye chiles, shallots, and garlic until they form a coarse paste.

2. Bring the broth to a gentle boil in a medium pot over medium-high or high heat. Reduce the heat to medium-low or medium, add the curry paste, and simmer for 2 to 3 minutes.

3. Add the fish sauce, kaffir lime leaves, chicken (if using raw), squash, mushrooms, and green beans and simmer 5 to 10 minutes, until the vegetables are tender and the chicken is cooked. Add the Chinese cabbage and simmer 1 to 2 minutes, until it wilts. If you are using cooked chicken, add it with the Chinese cabbage.

4. Turn off the heat and add the scallions, dill, and Thai basil. Stir to combine thoroughly.

5. Ladle the soup into individual bowls and season with the fish sauce, Thai basil, scallions, and lime juice to taste. (Alternatively, you may use any combination of those to suit your own tastes.) Serve with a side of jasmine rice (if using).

Pork Spareribs Hot and Sour Soup

Tom Saap

Makes 6 to 8 servings

This soup is about as easy as it gets and really showcases the fragrant depths that fresh lemongrass, galangal, and kaffir lime leaves can add to soups. It was one of the few soups for this book that I nailed on my first attempt when I was testing the recipes. It was so flavorful that I even surprised myself. To make sure I wasn't deceiving myself, I asked a friend who had just stopped by to give it a taste. The look on his face after that first spoonful told me everything I needed to know. His eyes closed, his head tilted back, his breath deepened, and he let out little groans of delight. I knew at that moment this recipe needed no further testing.

I like this recipe best with a light and clear broth, though richer broths are common too. For a light broth, using water as a base is preferable to a previously made pork broth as the pork ribs will create a light broth upon simmering. The seasonings here really bring everything together at the end. As this is typically a hot and sour soup, lime juice and chiles are often added liberally. If you love spicy, add some freshly chopped bird's eye chiles with the kaffir lime leaves. Otherwise, just add some chile flakes at the end, to taste, along with the lime juice and other seasonings.

Ingredients

1 pound pork spareribs, cut across the bone into 2-inch pieces

2 quarts water or pork bone broth (pages 47-51)

2 stalks lemongrass, cut into ¼-inch pieces (page 23)

1 (2-inch) piece fresh galangal, cut into ⅛- to ¼-inch slices

3 to 4 cloves garlic, finely chopped

2 small shallots, finely chopped

8 to 10 kaffir lime leaves, ripped in half

Cooked jasmine rice, for serving (optional)

Seasonings, to Taste

Fish sauce

Fresh chiles, thinly sliced

Chile powder

Fresh Thai basil leaves, coarsely chopped

Fresh lime juice

Directions

1. Add the spareribs and water to a large stockpot, bring the water to a gentle boil over high heat, and skim off any "scum" that forms on the surface before the water boils. Once the water boils, reduce the heat to medium-low or medium. Add the lemongrass, galangal, garlic, and shallots and simmer for about 1 hour, until the spareribs are tender.

2. During the last 10 minutes of cooking, add the kaffir lime leaves.

3. Ladle the soup into bowls and season with the fish sauce, chiles, chile powder, Thai basil, and lime juice to taste. (Alternatively, you may use any combination of those to suit your own tastes.)

4. Serve with a side of jasmine rice (if using).

Stuffed Bitter Melon Soup

Gaeng Jued Mara

Makes 6 to 8 servings

Bitter melon is a fruit that's found throughout Asia and Africa. There are different types of bitter melons, but generally speaking, they're about a foot long with an oblong shape and a green, bumpy, wrinkled exterior with a soft, fleshy white interior. You'll find them in the produce section of most Asian supermarkets.

Now, just a little warning about this recipe. Bitter melons are aptly named because they can be, well, *really* bitter. Some people love the taste while others hate it. If you've never tried bitter melon, I can testify that it's an acquired taste that gets better with time.

Another reason to give bitter melon a chance is that there are many known health benefits of bitter melon. In particular, bitter flavors are known to stimulate digestion and encourage the flow of saliva, bile, digestive enzymes, and stomach acid, all of which are essential for proper digestion. In fact, a trip to your local health food store will reveal dozens of tinctures of bitter medicinal plants known as "digestive bitters." Herbalists around the world, especially those from Ayurvedic and Chinese healing traditions, have used bitter melon for centuries for a wide range of digestive ailments. In recent decades, over one hundred studies have substantiated its healing effects for not just digestive issues but also for things like lowering blood sugar, reducing infections, boosting immunity, and even protecting against cancer.[28]

Ingredients

Pork Stuffing

½ pound ground pork

2 cloves garlic, minced

½ small onion or shallot, finely chopped

Pinch ground white pepper

2 tablespoons fish sauce or soy sauce

1 teaspoon coconut sugar (optional)

Soup

2 small to medium bitter melons

2 quarts pork or chicken bone broth (pages 47-51)

Cooked jasmine rice, for serving (optional)

Seasonings, to Taste

Fish sauce or soy sauce

Chile powder

Coconut sugar

Fresh cilantro leaves, coarsely chopped

Fresh Thai basil leaves, coarsely chopped

Directions

1. In a medium bowl, combine the ground pork, garlic, onion, pepper, fish sauce, and coconut sugar (if using). Set aside.

2. Blanch the bitter melons in boiling water for 1 minute. Remove them from the water and set them aside to cool. (Blanching the melons will reduce the bitterness slightly. You can skip this part if you really love intensely bitter flavor.)

3. Slice the bitter melons crosswise into about 1- to 1½-inch thick pieces. Core out the spongy white inner flesh with a spoon or paring knife.

4. Stuff the pork mixture into each piece of melon.

5. Bring the broth to a gentle boil in a large stockpot over high heat and add the stuffed melon pieces. Reduce the heat to medium-low or medium and simmer 15 to 20 minutes, until the pork is cooked through and the melon is tender.

6. Ladle the soup into individual bowls and season with the fish sauce, chile powder, coconut sugar, cilantro, and Thai basil to taste. (Alternatively, you may use any combination of those to suit your own tastes.)

7. Serve with a side of jasmine rice (if using).

Hot and Sour Fish Soup

Tom Yum Pla Nam Sai

Makes 3 to 4 servings

If you ever get a chance to travel to Bangkok, don't miss out on a trip to Chinatown, especially at night when the main street, Yaowarat Road, comes alive with a diverse array of food stalls and makeshift restaurants. At one intersection, there are two very popular competing seafood places, side-by-side, that spill out onto the street and are jam-packed all night long. It's the only place in Thailand I ever had to wait in line for a considerable time. And, boy, is it worth it both for the incredible fresh seafood and the experience of eating in such a frenetic, fast-paced street-side atmosphere.

It was on Yaowarat Road that I first had this hot and sour fish soup. Now technically, it wasn't really a soup. It was served as a steamed whole-fish dish in a hot and sour sauce (in Thai it's called *pla kapong neung manao*) with lots of chiles, lime, and garlic. It's kind of a quasi-soup dish. But it's easily transformed into a soup by adding some chicken or fish broth and using a fish fillet. Red snapper and barramundi are commonly used in Thailand, but you can use any type of fish you want.

Now, just a warning—this is typically a fiery hot dish. I went through an entire roll of toilet paper during that first meal. Yes, toilet paper. But no, not for that reason. Rolls of toilet paper are often used instead of paper napkins on the streets of Thailand. And, man, did the sinuses flow. If you ever find you've added too many chiles, add a touch more palm sugar and serve it with a side of jasmine rice. This will help diffuse the heat. Of course, you can tweak this recipe to your preferred degree of spiciness. I find one bird's eye chile is plenty of heat, but you could add a lot more. Exclude the chiles completely if you want.

Finally, feel free to play around with the amounts of garlic, shallots, chiles, sugar, lime juice, and fish sauce. As with all these recipes, nothing is set in stone.

Ingredients

- 1 tablespoon palm oil or coconut oil
- 2 small shallots or 1 small onion, minced, or more to taste
- 1 quart fish or chicken bone broth (pages 47-51)
- 2 stalks lemongrass, cut into ¼-inch thick slices (page 23)
- 1 (1-inch) piece fresh galangal, cut into ⅛- to ¼-inch thick slices
- 6 to 7 cloves garlic, minced, or more to taste
- 1 to 3 bird's eye chiles, sliced into thin rings, or more to taste
- 2 tablespoons fresh lime juice, or more to taste
- 2 teaspoons fish sauce, or more to taste
- 1 teaspoon palm sugar or coconut sugar, or more to taste
- 1 (1-pound) red snapper, cod, haddock, swordfish, or salmon fillet
- Cooked jasmine rice, for serving (optional)

Seasonings, to Taste

Fish sauce

Bird's eye chiles, thinly sliced

Chile powder

Coconut sugar

Fresh cilantro, coarsely chopped

Scallions, finely chopped

Fresh lime juice

Directions

1. In a large stockpot, heat the oil over medium heat. Add the shallots and sauté for 2 to 3 minutes.

2. Add the broth, lemongrass, galangal, garlic, and bird's eye chiles and simmer over medium heat for about 10 minutes. (If you desire more spiciness, add another chile or two.)

3. Add the lime juice, fish sauce, and palm sugar. Taste the soup and adjust as needed. A hot and sour flavor should predominate.

4. Add the fish fillet and simmer for 2 to 3 minutes, or until the fish is cooked through.

5. Ladle the soup into individual bowls and season with the fish sauce, bird's eye chiles, chile powder, coconut sugar, cilantro, scallions, and lime juice to taste. (Alternatively, you may use any combination of those to suit your own tastes.)

6. Serve with a side of jasmine rice (if using).

Thai Omelet Soup

Tom Jued Kai Num

Makes 3 to 4 servings

I know what you're thinking. Omelet in a soup? Really? Yup, it's a thing in Thailand. And it's as simple as adding an omelet to a simmering pot of broth seasoned with Thai herbs and spices. And, yes, it's delicious. If you're short on time and need an even simpler recipe than the one below, you can exclude the pork meatballs and the garlic paste. But I love the paste for the added aroma and flavor, and the meatballs make this a truly substantial meal. Finish it off with some generous splashes of fish sauce and a heaping spoonful or two of crunchy fried garlic and you'll never look at a plain omelet the same way again.

Ingredients

Pork Meatballs

½ pound ground pork

1 tablespoon fish sauce or soy sauce

Omelet

3 to 4 medium eggs

1 tablespoon fish sauce or soy sauce

2 to 3 tablespoons coconut oil or palm oil

Garlic Paste

3 to 4 cloves garlic

1 teaspoon whole black or white peppercorns

¼ cup loosely packed fresh cilantro stems, cut into ½-inch pieces

1 tablespoon coconut oil or palm oil

Soup

1 quart chicken or pork bone broth (pages 47-51)

1 tablespoon fish sauce

2 cups loosely packed chopped green cabbage, Chinese cabbage, or bok choy

2 small tomatoes, coarsely chopped

2 to 3 scallions, thinly sliced

½ cup loosely packed fresh cilantro

Cooked jasmine rice, for serving (optional)

Seasonings, to Taste

Fish sauce or soy sauce

Fried garlic

Scallions, finely chopped

Fresh cilantro, coarsely chopped

Directions

1. In a medium bowl, combine the ground pork and fish sauce. Set aside.
2. To make the omelet, combine the eggs and fish sauce in a small bowl and whisk together. Heat the coconut oil in a medium to large skillet over medium heat. Pour the egg mixture into the skillet and fry for 3 to 4 minutes, or until lightly browned, being careful not to burn it. Flip the omelet and lightly brown the other side. Set aside.
3. Using a mortar and pestle or a food processor, pound or blend the garlic, peppercorns, and cilantro stems into a paste. Heat the coconut oil in a medium pot over medium heat and sauté the paste for 2 minutes, stirring frequently.
4. Add the broth and fish sauce to the paste and bring the mixture to a simmer. Form small meatballs with the ground pork mixture, add them to the broth, and simmer 3 to 4 minutes until the meatballs are cooked through.
5. Add the cabbage and tomatoes and simmer for 2 to 3 more minutes.
6. Slice the omelet into bite-size pieces and add them to the soup. Add the scallions and cilantro and stir to combine.
7. Ladle the soup into individual bowls and season with the fish sauce, fried garlic, scallions, and cilantro to taste. (Alternatively, you may use any combination of those to suit your own tastes.)
8. Serve with a side of jasmine rice (if using).

THAI NOODLE SOUPS

Bone broth on wheels: that's what I call the noodle-soup carts of Thailand. They're found *everywhere*, roaming through the streets of cities and towns or parked at roadside stalls and markets. In the middle of the cart is a large stockpot, about 1½–2 feet in diameter and maybe 3–4 feet deep. Within the stockpot are three separate chambers, two for a few different types of broth and a third smaller one for boiling and blanching various noodles and veggies. Next to the stockpot is a small display window showcasing different types of noodles, veggies, herbs, chiles, meats, pastes, and sauces, all of which are added to the broth in different ways to create a variety of different soups.

> **Thai Noodle-Soup Carts**
>
> If you're curious what the noodle-soup carts look and sound like, you can see some videos of them on YouTube. In the search field, type in something like "Thai noodle soup street food" or "Thai noodle soup street vendor," and you'll see what I've just described in these pages.

You'll often hear the noodle-soup carts coming, too, as the vendors will tap two pieces of bamboo block together, creating a resonant sound that's often referred to as *pok pok*. This lets people know that noodle soup is nearby. Just the thought of that sound makes me start salivating!

These noodle soups are an iconic part of Thai street food and culture, offering an almost infinite variety of different styles and flavors that blend influences from throughout Asia. While some have evolved into uniquely Thai versions, some are not so different from what you might find in other Southeast Asian countries. For example, the famous Vietnamese noodle soup, pho, is not that different from Thai beef noodle soups.

Regardless of the type of soup, these noodle-soup carts always serve up some variety of pork, beef, or chicken broths (with pork probably being the most common), and each vendor creates their own uniquely flavored broth.

In the three recipes that follow, I've attempted to highlight some common differences between the different types of noodle soups found in Thailand. For example, the broth in the beef noodle soup is complex, rich, slightly sweet, and flavored with cinnamon and star anise. The chicken noodle soup uses a light broth but is seasoned with a paste of cilantro, black pepper, and garlic, which infuses the broth with a subtle but noticeable spice. And the pork noodle soup is fairly straightforward but is seasoned with crushed peanuts and fried garlic to give it a smoky, nutty flavor that fuses well with the pork broth.

Also, I've kept the cuts of meat very simple in these recipes. For the beef, use any tender cut of raw beef and slice it into very thin strips. You could also flash-fry the beef in some oil on both sides and then slice it thinly. Simply pouring the hot broth over the strips will cook them sufficiently. For the chicken and pork, simply use any cut you want. You can cook it and then slice it into strips or cubes; or, you can use a raw piece of meat, slice it thinly, and simmer it a few minutes in the broth to cook it through. This latter method will often result in somewhat tougher meat, but this is actually a common method in Thailand.

In Thailand and throughout Asia, you'll also see cuts like tendons and shank, which are slowly simmered in the broth to break down the tough fibers. These cuts also add different textures and flavors too. Organ meats are also very common, especially with pork. I've chosen to avoid these, because I know they're unfamiliar to most Americans—but if you're okay with them, by all means, go for it.

Also, for the purposes of keeping things gluten-free, I only use rice noodles in these recipes. However, most noodle soups in Thailand are Chinese in origin, and many (especially pork-based soups) do use egg and wheat noodles. You could certainly substitute something like lo mein, chow mein, or wonton noodles if you're not intolerant to gluten. Just be forewarned that a lot of egg noodles, both fresh and dried, contain many chemical flavorings and colors.

Thai Beef Noodle Soup

Kuay Teow Neua

Makes 6 to 8 servings

Before Bangkok became a modern industrial metropolis, it was actually known as the "Venice of the East," with an extensive network of canals and floating markets. Sadly, these are now mostly paved over. But you can still taste the past in the form of Bangkok's famous boat noodles, a beef noodle soup that was once served from the boats that traversed the canals (there are pork versions of this dish as well). Although there are many types of beef noodle soups in Thailand, boat noodles soup is probably the most well-known and is the inspiration for this recipe.

Boat noodles' defining feature is the intensely flavorful broth that's simmered for many hours in aromatic herbs and spices. A dark and sweet soy sauce—as well as a little sugar—gives it an added robust sweetness. It certainly resembles Vietnam's iconic beef noodle soup, pho, but the triple gem–infused broth gives it a unique Thai flavor.

Another uniquely Thai aspect of this soup is the traditional addition of blood, which is used for added richness and flavor. Don't worry, I haven't included it in this recipe. I know it sounds crazy, but blood is a common ingredient in traditional soups all around the world. If you're feeling adventurous, stir in a teaspoon or two of beef blood just before adding the seasonings. You can ask your local butcher for this or you might even find it sold in Asian markets.

Finally, if you ever make it to Bangkok, make sure to visit the Victory Monument area, where there's a boatload (sorry, I couldn't resist) of boat noodle places serving up the real thing.

Ingredients

Beef Broth

- 2 quarts beef bone broth (pages 47-51)
- 2 stalks lemongrass, cut into 1- to 2-inch thick pieces (page 23)
- 1 (2-inch) piece fresh galangal, cut into coarse slices
- 8 to 10 kaffir lime leaves, whole or ripped in half
- 3 to 4 cloves garlic, finely chopped
- ½ medium onion, 2 to 3 small shallots, or 3 to 4 scallions, finely chopped
- 3 to 4 whole star anise
- 1 (2-inch) cinnamon stick
- ½ teaspoon whole black peppercorns
- 2 tablespoons black soy sauce (see sidebar)
- 1 tablespoon palm sugar or coconut sugar

> **What Is Black Soy Sauce?**
>
> Black soy sauce is a thick type of soy sauce that is made with sugar or molasses and thus has a salty and sweet flavor. It pairs well with many types of noodle soups. You'll find it in Asian markets. If you prefer to keep this soup gluten-free, substitute the black soy sauce with a gluten-free soy sauce or ¼ cup full-bodied red wine.

Soup

1 (14-ounce) package rice noodles

3 to 4 cups spinach, bok choy, or kale, stemmed

1 pound tenderloin or strip steak (or any other tender cut of beef), sliced against the grain into very thin strips

Seasonings, to Taste

Fish sauce or Chiles in Fish Sauce (page 33)

Fresh chiles or Chiles in Vinegar (page 34)

Chile powder

Coconut sugar

Scallions, finely chopped

Fresh bean sprouts

Fresh cilantro, coarsely chopped

Fresh Thai basil leaves, coarsely chopped

Fresh lime juice

Directions

1. Gently simmer the broth with the lemongrass, galangal, kaffir lime leaves, garlic, onion, star anise, cinnamon, peppercorns, soy sauce, and palm sugar in a large pot over medium-low heat for 2 to 3 hours to let the flavors marry. Strain out all the solid ingredients.

2. Prepare the rice noodles according to package directions and set aside.

3. Just before the beef broth is finished simmering, add the spinach to the broth to gently wilt it for 2 to 3 minutes.

4. To individual bowls, add a handful or two of the cooked rice noodles and raw tenderloin strips. Ladle a few cups of hot broth over the noodles and beef, and let the bowls sit for 1 to 2 minutes to cook the meat. Season with the fish sauce, chiles, chile powder, coconut sugar, scallions, bean sprouts, cilantro, Thai basil, and lime juice to taste. (Alternatively, you may use any combination of those to suit your own tastes.)

Thai Chicken Noodle Soup

Kuay Teow Gai

Makes 3 to 4 servings

This recipe is not that different from a chicken noodle soup your grandmother would make. The major difference is the broth, which has the added depths of flavor from the garlic-peppercorn-cilantro paste and the triple gem of Thai aromatics. This combination makes so much flavor that I'd wager you'll like this chicken noodle soup even more than your grandmother's version. Don't take offense to that. I know people get very defensive when it comes to their grandmother's cooking. I'm sure your grandmother is a great cook. Just make this Thai version and get back to me.

Ingredients

Garlic-Peppercorn-Cilantro Paste

3 to 4 cloves garlic

1 teaspoon whole black peppercorns

¼ cup packed fresh cilantro stems, cut into ½-inch pieces

1 tablespoon coconut oil or palm oil

Soup

1 quart chicken bone broth (pages 47-51)

1 stalk lemongrass, cut into ¼-inch thick slices (page 23)

1 (1-inch) piece fresh galangal, cut into ⅛- to ¼-inch thick slices

3 to 4 kaffir lime leaves, ripped in half

2 teaspoons fish sauce

1 (14-ounce) package rice noodles

1 cup shredded or cubed cooked chicken

Seasonings, to Taste

Fish sauce or Chiles in Fish Sauce (page 33)

Fresh chiles or Chiles in Vinegar (page 34)

Chile powder

Coconut sugar

Fresh bean sprouts

Fresh Thai basil leaves, coarsely chopped

Fresh lime juice

Directions

1. Using a mortar and pestle or a food processor, pound or blend together the garlic, peppercorns, and cilantro stems until they form a paste.

2. Heat the oil in a medium pot over medium heat and sauté the paste for 2 minutes, stirring frequently.

3. Add the broth, lemongrass, galangal, kaffir lime leaves, and fish sauce to the paste. Bring the mixture to a boil, then reduce the heat to medium-low or medium and simmer for 10 to 15 minutes.

4. While the broth is simmering, prepare the rice noodles according to package directions and set aside.

5. Add a handful of noodles and chicken to individual bowls and ladle the broth over them. Season with the fish sauce, chiles, chile powder, coconut sugar, bean sprouts, Thai basil, and lime juice to taste. (Alternatively, you may use any combination of those to suit your own tastes.)

Thai Pork Noodle Soup

Kuay Teow Moo

Makes 3 to 4 servings

There are so many different types of pork noodle soups in Thailand that one could easily write a book on just pork noodle soups. Every type of noodle, vegetable, herb, and spice and every possible cut of pork (including entrails) are used for endless varieties. This recipe is a good starting point from which to improvise your own pork noodle soup. And don't be shy about customizing the soup at the end. Remember, noodle soups make a great vehicle for using the quintessential Thai seasonings of Chiles in Fish Sauce and Chiles in Vinegar (pages 33-34). For me, fried garlic, peanuts, and Thai basil are an absolute *must*.

Ingredients

1 pound pork shoulder, pork loin, or pork cutlets (or any other boneless piece of pork)

1 (14-ounce) package rice noodles

1 quart pork or chicken bone broth (pages 47-51)

1 to 2 tablespoons fish sauce, or to taste

1 to 2 cups tightly packed Chinese celery, bok choy, Chinese cabbage, spinach, mustard greens, or kale leaves

Seasonings, to Taste

Fish sauce or Chiles in Fish Sauce (page 33)

Fresh chiles or Chiles in Vinegar (page 34)

Chile powder

Coconut sugar

Fried garlic

Fresh bean sprouts

Raw or roasted unsalted peanuts, crushed

Scallions, finely chopped

Fresh Thai basil leaves, coarsely chopped

Directions

1. Cook the pork any way you want (roasting or grilling brings out additional flavors), then slice or chop it into thin pieces.

2. While the pork is cooking, prepare the rice noodles according to package directions and set aside.

3. Bring the broth and fish sauce to a gentle boil in a medium pot over medium-high or high heat and add the greens. Reduce the heat to medium-low or medium and simmer 1 to 2 minutes, or until the greens are gently wilted.

4. Place the noodles and pork in individual bowls and ladle the broth and greens over them. Season with the fish sauce, chiles, chile powder, coconut sugar, fried garlic, bean sprouts, peanuts, scallions, and Thai basil to taste. (Alternatively, you may use any combination of those to suit your own tastes.)

CHAPTER 11
Thai Fusion Soups: Fun and Creative Inspirations From Around the World

A first-rate soup is more creative than a second-rate painting.
—Abraham Maslow

It is not hard to see why Thai cuisine has become so popular outside Thailand. Traditional Thai flavors and ingredients lend themselves well to blending with other cuisines. Creative chefs around the world have been fusing Western cuisine with the salty, sour, sweet, and spicy flavors of Thai foods for decades with fantastic results. In my opinion, no place is this easier to do than with soup, as I consider broth the ultimate medium for improvisation and experimentation.

For example, you can take almost any typical creamy vegetable soup, substitute coconut milk or coconut cream for dairy-based milk or cream, and throw in some Thai seasonings for a Thai-inspired fusion soup. Broth-based soups can be even easier mediums in which to find exciting combinations—just tinker with the ingredients. Things like lime juice, fish sauce, and even chiles can be simple substitutions or additions to enhance and tweak recipes.

Think of the soup recipes that your mother or grandmother used to make. Think of the soup recipes that are part of your ethnic heritage. There are probably quite a few that can easily be fused into a Thai version. The ten recipes here are a great starting point to illustrate how easy and fun fusion cuisine can be.

In time, you might even come up with your own unique fusion recipe that becomes a standard part of your soup-making repertoire. The first recipe in this chapter is a good example of that in my own life.

Thai Basil Pesto Soup with Shrimp

If you're skimming through the recipes in this book, looking for one you'd really like to try, stop right here. Do not turn the page. Trust me, this is the one. This is my favorite fusion recipe and the one I believe has the broadest appeal to my people because my people *love* a good pesto. I've never met anyone who didn't like a sauce of fresh basil blended with pine nuts, garlic, and olive oil mixed in a warm, wheaty bed of angel hair pasta.

This Thai soup version isn't that much of a departure from that classic Italian pasta dish. The big differences are the use of Thai basil in place of sweet basil, peanuts in place of pine nuts, and vermicelli rice noodles in place of angel hair pasta. And, of course, this recipe employs a triple gem–infused broth. I don't know why it works so beautifully, but sometimes it's best not to try to explain why. Just make this and you'll understand.

I love the jalapeño in this soup for the little bit of heat it adds, but you could leave it out (or add a spicier chile). And feel free to substitute a different nut if needed. Peanuts are ideal to use, as they're a traditional Thai ingredient—and a lot cheaper than pine nuts—but pestos can be made with almost any type of seed or nut, including sunflower seeds, almonds, cashews, and walnuts.

Finally, the broth-to-noodle ratio is entirely up to you. Add just a little broth for more of a noodle dish and add a lot of broth for more of a soup. I like it somewhere in between. The more broth you add, the more pesto you'll need, as the broth will dilute the pesto a bit. Add more pesto to taste and don't be afraid to season generously at the end. Lime juice, fish sauce, and peanuts really round everything out. And though I think this pairs perfectly with shrimp, other types of seafood (or chicken) would work well too.

Ingredients

Pesto

Makes about 1 cup

- 2 cups tightly packed fresh Thai basil leaves
- ½ cup unsalted roasted peanuts
- 2 to 3 cloves garlic
- 2 tablespoons fish sauce
- 2 tablespoons lime juice
- 1 jalapeño, seeded (optional)
- ½ cup olive oil

Soup

1 quart fish or chicken bone broth (pages 47-54)

1 stalk lemongrass, cut into ¼-inch thick slices (page 23)

1 (1-inch) piece fresh galangal, cut into ⅛- to ¼-inch thick slices

3 to 4 kaffir lime leaves, ripped in half

1 (14-ounce) package vermicelli rice noodles

½ pound shrimp, shelled

Seasonings, to Taste

Fish sauce

Fresh chiles, thinly sliced, or chile powder

Unsalted roasted peanuts, crushed

Fresh lime juice

Directions

1. To make the pesto, place the Thai basil, peanuts, garlic, fish sauce, lime juice, and jalapeño into a food processor and pulse until thoroughly blended. Then add the olive oil in a thin, steady stream while the food processor's blade is running until the mixture forms a paste.

2. Bring the broth to a boil in a medium stockpot over high heat. Reduce the heat to medium-low or medium and add the lemongrass, galangal, and kaffir lime leaves and simmer for 10 to 15 minutes.

3. While the broth is simmering, prepare the vermicelli according to package directions and set aside.

4. Add the shrimp to the broth and simmer for 1 to 2 minutes, or until the shrimp are cooked through.

5. Add a handful of noodles to individual bowls. Add about 1 tablespoon of the pesto, mix well, and taste. Add more pesto if needed. Ladle 1 or 2 cups broth over the noodles, taste, and add more broth and pesto, if desired. Season with the fish sauce, chiles, peanuts, and lime juice to taste. (Alternatively, you may use any combination of those to suit your own tastes.)

6. Top each serving with the cooked shrimp.

Thai Creamy Coconut Carrot Soup

Makes 4 to 5 servings

In my book *Fearless Broths and Soups*, I threw in a creamy vegetable soup chapter only because I know they're familiar to most people. Whether your mother made them from scratch or you had them in heavily processed canned form, we all grew up with things like cream of tomato, potato, broccoli, and so on. Truth be told, they're my least favorite soups. I just find them, well, kind of boring. But I think Thai versions are more conducive to variations using coconut milk in place of cow's milk; in addition, they're perfect for experimenting with different combos of salty, sweet, and sour seasonings. This recipe is a great example.

For me, it's all about finding that perfect consistency of sweet carrots, creamy rich coconut milk, and savory chicken broth with Thai herbs. Add a little more broth for a thinner consistency or little less broth and a tad more coconut milk (or even coconut cream) for a thicker, richer flavor. I prefer the latter mixed with a little lime juice, a dash of fish sauce, a pinch of chile powder, and some chopped Thai basil.

Ingredients

- 1 tablespoon coconut oil
- 2 small shallots or 1 medium onion, minced
- 3 to 4 cloves garlic, minced
- 1 (1-inch) piece fresh galangal or ginger, cut into ⅛- to ¼-inch thick slices
- 2 stalks lemongrass, cut into ¼-inch thick slices (page 23)
- 1 quart chicken bone broth (pages 47-51)
- 1 pound carrots, peeled and cut into ¼-inch thick rounds
- 4 to 5 whole kaffir lime leaves
- 1 tablespoon fish sauce
- 1 (14-ounce) can full-fat coconut milk
- 1 bird's eye chile, sliced in half and seeded (optional)
- ¼ cup tightly packed fresh cilantro, coarsely chopped

Seasonings, to Taste

- Fish sauce or soy sauce
- Fresh chiles, thinly sliced, or chile powder
- Fresh cilantro, coarsely chopped
- Fresh Thai basil leaves, coarsely chopped
- Freshly ground black or white pepper
- Fresh lime juice

Directions

1. Heat the coconut oil in a medium to large stockpot over medium heat. Add the shallots, garlic, galangal, and lemongrass and sauté for about 2 to 3 minutes, or until the mixture is fragrant.
2. Add the broth and bring the mixture to a boil. Add the carrots, kaffir lime leaves, and fish sauce and reduce the heat to medium-low. Cover the stockpot and simmer until the carrots are tender, stirring occasionally, about 10 to 15 minutes.
3. Add the coconut milk, bird's eye chile (if using), and cilantro and simmer another 5 to 10 minutes.
4. Remove and discard the lemongrass, galangal, kaffir lime leaves, and bird's eye chile.
5. Puree the soup with an immersion blender.
6. Ladle the soup into individual bowls and season with the fish sauce, chiles, cilantro, Thai basil, pepper, and lime juice to taste. (Alternatively, you may use any combination of those to suit your own tastes.)

Thai Bouillabaisse

Makes 3 to 4 servings

If there was ever a match made in heaven, I think it would have to be a French bouillabaisse and a tom yum soup. A light seafood broth swimming with fresh fish and shellfish, infused with lemongrass, galangal, kaffir lime, and chiles and seasoned with lime juice, herbs, and fish sauce is about as divine as it gets. If you're a seafood lover, this is the recipe for you.

Ingredients

- 1 tablespoon olive oil
- 1 small shallot or onion, minced
- 2 to 3 cloves garlic, minced
- 1 jalapeño, seeded and minced
- 1 quart fish broth (page 52) or water
- 2 stalks lemongrass, cut into ¼-inch thick slices (page 23)
- 1 (1- to 2-inch) piece fresh galangal or ginger, cut into ⅛- to ¼-inch thick slices
- 4 to 5 kaffir lime leaves, ripped in half
- 1 to 2 tablespoons fish sauce
- 1 to 2 tablespoons fresh lime juice
- ½ pound cod, halibut, or snapper, cubed
- 8 to 12 medium to large shrimp, shelled
- 8 to 12 clams (any variety)
- 8 to 12 mussels (any size)
- ¼ cup loosely packed fresh Thai basil leaves, coarsely chopped
- ¼ cup loosely packed fresh cilantro, coarsely chopped

Seasonings, to Taste

- Fish sauce
- Fresh chiles, thinly sliced
- Fresh Thai basil leaves, coarsely chopped
- Fresh cilantro, coarsely chopped
- Fresh lime juice
- Salt and freshly ground black pepper

Directions

1. In a medium stockpot, heat the oil over medium heat. Add the shallot, garlic, and jalapeño and sauté for about 5 minutes.

2. Add the broth, lemongrass, galangal, and kaffir lime leaves and simmer for 10 to 15 minutes.

3. Add 1 tablespoon of the fish sauce and 1 tablespoon of the lime juice, taste the soup, and add the remaining 1 tablespoon fish sauce and 1 tablespoon lime juice, if needed.

4. Add the cod, shrimp, clams, mussels, Thai basil, and cilantro and simmer until the mussels and clams open, about 5 to 10 minutes.

5. Ladle the soup into bowls and season with the fish sauce, chiles, Thai basil, cilantro, lime juice, and salt and pepper to taste. (Alternatively, you may use any combination of those to suit your own tastes.)

Thai Mango Gazpacho

Makes 3 to 4 servings

Native to southern Spain, gazpacho is probably the world's most famous cold soup. It has spread around the world with a zillion incarnations, though most have some combination of tomatoes, onion, garlic, and peppers. This Thai version is the best one I've ever had. Juicy mangoes, refreshing lime juice, cooling mint, sweet Thai basil, zesty chile peppers, and fresh veggies all blended together is pretty magical stuff, especially on a hot and steamy summer day. But make sure the mangoes are ripe—that's the key in this recipe. Squeeze them to make sure they're soft, like a ripe avocado or peach, before you slice them. Even slightly unripe mangoes will prevent this recipe from hitting its sweet peak.

Ingredients

- 2 mangoes, peeled and pitted
- 1 cup cherry tomatoes
- 1 medium red bell pepper
- ½ medium red onion
- 2 cloves garlic
- 1 medium cucumber, peeled
- 1 jalapeño
- 2 to 3 tablespoons fresh cilantro
- 2 to 3 tablespoons fresh mint
- 2 to 3 tablespoons fresh lime juice
- 1 tablespoon fish sauce

Seasonings, to Taste

- Fish sauce
- Chile powder
- Fresh mint, coarsely chopped
- Fresh Thai basil leaves, coarsely chopped
- Fresh lime juice

> **Smooth or Chunky?**
>
> As far as the consistency of this soup goes, I love a chunkier texture with big pieces of mango. You might not, and that's totally fine. Gazpacho can be as smooth or as chunky as you like. Blend it according to your own desires.

Directions

1. Cut the mangoes into small pieces. Finely chop the cherry tomatoes, bell pepper, onion, garlic, cucumber, jalapeño, cilantro, and mint and transfer them to a large bowl. Add the lime juice and fish sauce and combine thoroughly.
2. Take about half of the mango mixture and blend it in a blender or food processor until smooth (see sidebar).
3. Return the pureed mango mixture to the bowl and stir to combine.
4. Ladle the soup into individual bowls and season with the fish sauce, chile powder, mint, Thai basil, and lime juice to taste. (Alternatively, you may use any combination of those to suit your own tastes.)

Thai-Mexican Meatball Soup

Makes 3 to 4 servings

Here's a simple Thai twist on the classic Mexican *sopa de albóndigas*, or *meatball soup*. *Albóndigas* is Spanish for *meatballs*, which are seasoned with lots of fresh herbs, garlic, and onion and cooked with raw rice to bind everything together (though this is totally optional). The soup itself is a tomato-based beef broth also seasoned with herbs and cooked with lots of vegetables. Rice can be added for a heartier version (also optional). In this recipe, I simply add some Thai elements to the meatballs and broth. It's not a dramatic departure from a traditional Mexican recipe, but as they say, sometimes less is more. All I know for sure is that this is some serious soul-soothing comfort food, especially when you add in some soft, buttery chunks of avocado.

Ingredients

Meatballs

½ pound ground beef

¼ cup uncooked jasmine rice (optional)

1 stalk lemongrass, bottom half thinly sliced and minced (page 23)

1 (1-inch) piece fresh ginger, peeled and minced

2 to 3 garlic cloves, minced

2 scallions, finely chopped

1 jalapeño, seeded and minced

2 tablespoons fresh cilantro, coarsely chopped

1 tablespoon fresh mint, coarsely chopped

1 tablespoon fish sauce

½ teaspoon salt

Soup

1 tablespoon olive oil

1 medium onion, finely chopped

1 medium green or red bell pepper, finely chopped

1 jalapeño, finely chopped

2 to 3 cloves garlic, finely chopped

1 quart beef bone broth (pages 47-51)

1 (14-ounce) can diced tomatoes, drained

2 to 3 tablespoons fresh lime juice, plus more to taste

½ cup uncooked jasmine rice (optional)

¼ cup fresh cilantro, coarsely chopped

Salt and freshly ground black or white pepper, to taste

Seasonings, to Taste

Fish sauce or salt

Fresh chiles, thinly sliced

Chile powder

Coarsely chopped avocado

Scallions, finely chopped

Fresh cilantro, coarsely chopped

Fresh lime juice

Directions

1. In a medium bowl, combine the ground beef, uncooked jasmine rice (if using), lemongrass, ginger, garlic, scallions, jalapeño, cilantro, mint, fish sauce, and salt. Form the mixture into bite-size balls and set them aside.

2. Heat the oil over medium heat in a medium to large stockpot. Add the onion, bell pepper, jalapeño, and garlic and sauté about 5 minutes. Add the broth, tomatoes, and lime juice and bring to a simmer.

3. Add the meatballs and simmer 30 to 40 minutes, until the meatballs are very tender. If using the uncooked rice, rinse it a few times in cold water and add it to the soup in the last 15 minutes of cooking.

4. Season the soup with additional lime juice, if desired, and the cilantro and salt and pepper.

5. Ladle the soup into bowls and season with the fish sauce, chiles, chile powder, avocado, scallions, cilantro, and lime juice to taste. (Alternatively, you may use any combination of those to suit your own tastes.)

Thai Watermelon-Mint Soup with Calamari Ceviche

Makes 3 to 4 servings

Surely, somewhere in Thailand someone makes a recipe similar to this one, though I never encountered it in my travels. The combination of Thai seasonings, mint, watermelon, and a hot summer day makes for a wonderfully cooling and intensely flavorful soup. Planning an outdoor backyard party in summer? Make this and watch the praise and love flow your way.

This recipe, as well as the Thai Mango Gazpacho (page 139), are the only soup recipes in this book that don't use bone broth, because both recipes create their own "broth" from the fruit juices. Both recipes are meant to be consumed cold.

For the calamari ceviche, you could easily substitute shrimp, scallops, crab, or a meaty fish like salmon or tuna for the squid.

Ingredients

Calamari Ceviche

- 1 pound raw or cooked squid (preferably raw), cut into ½-inch thick rings with tentacles left whole
- 1 tablespoon olive oil
- 1 tablespoon red wine vinegar or apple cider vinegar
- 1 medium red onion or 2 small shallots, finely chopped
- 1 jalapeño or serrano, finely chopped
- 2 to 3 tablespoons fresh cilantro, finely chopped
- 2 tablespoons fresh lime juice
- Pinch sugar, or to taste
- Salt and freshly ground black pepper, to taste

Soup

- 4 cups cubed watermelon
- 1 tablespoon olive oil
- 1 stalk lemongrass, bottom half thinly sliced and minced (page 23)
- 1 (1-inch) piece fresh galangal or ginger, peeled and minced
- 2 to 3 cloves garlic, finely chopped
- 1 to 2 serranos or jalapeños
- 4 to 5 kaffir lime leaves, ripped in half
- 1 teaspoon fish sauce, plus more to taste
- 1 tablespoon fresh lime juice, plus more to taste
- 2 tablespoons fresh mint, coarsely chopped, plus more to taste

Seasonings, to Taste

Fish sauce

Fresh chiles, thinly sliced, or chile powder

Fresh mint, coarsely chopped

Fresh lime juice

Directions

1. If you are using raw squid, blanch the rings and tentacles in boiling water for 1 minute. Drain the squid and submerge it in cold water to stop the cooking process. Drain the squid from the cold water and set aside.

2. In a medium bowl, combine the oil, vinegar, onion, jalapeño, cilantro, and lime juice. Add the sugar and salt and pepper. Add the squid, stir to combine, and set the bowl in the fridge for at least 1 hour to chill.

3. Blend the watermelon in a blender or food processor until liquefied. Set aside.

4. Heat the oil in a medium to large stockpot over medium heat. Add the lemongrass, galangal, garlic, and serranos and sauté for 5 to 10 minutes, until the mixture is fragrant. Add half the watermelon juice and the kaffir lime leaves and simmer 5 to 10 minutes. Discard the kaffir lime leaves after simmering and add the fish sauce, lime juice, and mint.

5. Blend this heated mixture in a blender or food processor until smooth. Add the remaining watermelon juice and blend again.

6. Taste the soup and add more fish sauce, lime juice, and mint if desired. Blend again.

7. Strain the soup into a large serving bowl and transfer it to the fridge to chill for about 2 hours.

8. Ladle the soup into individual bowls, top each serving with the calamari ceviche, and season with the fish sauce, chiles, mint, and lime juice to taste. (Alternatively, you may use any combination of those to suit your own tastes.)

Thai Cilantro-Mint Pesto Soup with Halibut

Makes 3 to 4 servings

Pestos don't always have to use basil and olive oil. Different herbs, oils, and nuts can offer fun and creative alternatives. In this case, cilantro, mint, roasted cashews, and sesame oil blended with some classic Thai seasonings create a bright and zesty pesto that's sure to perk up your taste buds.

I love this soup in late summer and early fall when fresh halibut is in season and the sweetness of local cherry tomatoes is at its peak. And though it's an extra step, grilling or roasting the halibut separately will add depth of flavor. And don't be shy about the seasoning! Personally, I think some generous dashes of fish sauce and lime juice really harmonize all the flavors in the end.

Ingredients

Pesto

2 cups tightly packed fresh cilantro with stems

¼ cup loosely packed fresh mint leaves

½ cup unsalted roasted cashews

1 stalk lemongrass, bottom half thinly sliced and minced (page 23)

3 to 4 cloves garlic

1 (1-inch) piece fresh ginger, finely chopped

1 to 2 jalapeños (optional)

2 tablespoons fresh lime juice

1 tablespoon fish sauce

½ cup sesame oil (not toasted)

Soup

1 (14-ounce) package vermicelli rice noodles

1 quart fish or chicken bone broth (pages 47-54)

1 cup cherry tomatoes, halved

1 medium red bell pepper, cut into ¼-inch thick strips

1 (½-pound) halibut fillet, cubed

Seasonings, to Taste

Fish sauce

Chile powder

Unsalted roasted cashews, crushed

Fresh lime juice

Directions

1. Combine the cilantro, mint, cashews, lemongrass, garlic, ginger, jalapeños (if using), lime juice, and fish sauce in a food processor and pulse until thoroughly blended. Add the sesame oil in a thin, steady stream while the food processor is running, until the mixture forms a paste.

2. Prepare the vermicelli rice noodles according to package directions. Rinse the cooked noodles in cool water and set aside.

3. Bring the broth to a gentle boil in a medium stockpot over medium-high or high heat. Add the cherry tomatoes and bell pepper and reduce the heat to medium-low or medium and simmer about 5 minutes. Add the halibut and simmer for 3 to 4 minutes, until the halibut is cooked through.

4. Place a handful of noodles in individual bowls and add about 1 tablespoon pesto. Mix well and taste. Add more pesto if needed. Spoon 1 or 2 cups soup over the noodles, taste, and add more broth and pesto, if desired. Season with the fish sauce, chile powder, cashews, and lime juice to taste. (Alternatively, you may use any combination of those to suit your own tastes.)

Thai-Portuguese Kale Soup

Makes 3 to 4 servings

Considering that the chile pepper was first introduced to Thailand by Portuguese traders in the sixteenth century, there's actually a lot these two cuisines have in common. The classic Portuguese kale soup typically uses chorizo sausage, which contains smoked dried red peppers. In this Thai version, I've substituted Thai-style pork meatballs, which include jalapeños or serranos—these give this recipe a little more zing. You could up the zing factor quite a bit by adding some chopped fresh bird's eye chiles at the end! I prefer some dried chile flakes instead. Whatever your "zing tolerance," infusing the broth with lemongrass and kaffir lime and then seasoning to taste with both lime juice and fish sauce rounds everything out to create a wonderful Thai-Portuguese fusion soup.

Ingredients

Pork Meatballs

- ½ pound ground pork
- 1 stalk lemongrass, bottom half thinly sliced and minced (page 23)
- 2 cloves garlic, minced
- 1 (1-inch) piece fresh ginger, peeled and minced
- 1 small shallot, minced
- ½ serrano or 1 jalapeño, minced
- 2 tablespoons fish sauce
- 2 tablespoons olive oil

Soup

- 1 tablespoon coconut oil, palm oil, or olive oil
- 1 medium onion, finely chopped
- 2 to 3 cloves garlic, finely chopped
- ½ serrano or 1 jalapeño, finely chopped
- 1 quart beef or pork bone broth (pages 47-51)
- 1 stalk lemongrass, cut into ¼-inch thick slices (page 23)
- 4 to 5 kaffir lime leaves, ripped in half
- 2 to 3 medium Yukon gold, red, or russet potatoes, cut into ½-inch cubes
- 1 large bunch kale, coarsely chopped

Seasonings, to Taste

- Fish sauce
- Fresh chiles
- Chile powder
- Fresh lime juice

Directions

1. Combine the ground pork, lemongrass, garlic, ginger, shallot, serrano, and fish sauce in a medium bowl. Let the mixture chill in the refrigerate for at least 1 hour or up to overnight.

2. To make the soup, heat the coconut oil in a large stockpot over medium heat. Add the onion, garlic, and serrano and sauté for about 5 minutes.

3. Add the broth, lemongrass, kaffir lime leaves, and potatoes and simmer for 10 to 15 minutes, or until the potatoes are tender.

4. While the broth is simmering, form bite-size meatballs with the pork mixture. Heat the olive oil in a medium skillet over medium heat and very briefly brown the meatballs on all sides, about 20 to 30 seconds per side. Set aside. (Don't overcook the meatballs, as they will cook further when added to the broth.)

5. When the potatoes are tender, add the kale and simmer 1 to 2 minutes, or until the kale is wilted. Add the meatballs and simmer 1 more minute.

6. Ladle the soup into individual bowls and season with the fish sauce, chiles, chile powder, and lime juice to taste. (Alternatively, you may use any combination of those to suit your own tastes.)

Sweet and Sour Green Chile-Garlic Soup

Makes 3 to 4 servings

The fresh fish, caught that day, were laid out on a bed of ice to entice passersby to stop and eat at the beachside cafe. Nearby, the hot coals were sizzling away as the sun dipped below the horizon on the Andaman Sea. A Thai woman was busy preparing a variety of colorful Thai pastes and sauces. Sensing my delight at all the succulent sights and smells, she asked me if I wanted to taste one of her pastes. I pointed to the bright green one. I knew right away what I was having for dinner that night. The sweet and sour green chile grilled snapper was as unforgettable a meal as I've ever had. I remember thinking that the paste might work well in a soup. When I got home to America and created this recipe, I found that my intuition was correct.

Ingredients

Sweet and Sour Green Chile–Garlic Paste

Makes about 1 cup

- 1 small bunch fresh cilantro
- 1 to 4 jalapeños or serranos (see sidebar)
- 4 to 5 cloves garlic
- 1 small bunch scallions or 2 to 3 small shallots
- 2 to 3 tablespoons coconut sugar
- 2 to 3 tablespoons fish sauce
- 3 to 4 tablespoons fresh lime juice

Soup

- 1 quart chicken bone broth (pages 47-51)
- 2 cups cooked jasmine rice
- 2 cups cooked cubed or shredded chicken
- 3 to 6 tablespoons Sweet and Sour Green Chile–Garlic Paste

Seasonings, to Taste

- Fish sauce
- Coconut sugar
- Fresh lime juice

Spice Levels and Chiles

Use one jalapeño or serrano for a mild spice level, two for a moderate spice level, three for a really good kick, and four for some serious spiciness. And remember, spice levels can vary even in the same types of chiles. You can't undo adding too many chiles to your soup! Always start with smaller amounts and add more, to personal taste.

Directions

1. Combine the cilantro, jalapeños, garlic, scallions, coconut sugar, fish sauce, and lime juice in a food processor and blend until the mixture forms a paste.

2. Bring the broth to a simmer in a medium to large stockpot over medium heat. Add the rice and chicken, then add 3 tablespoons of the green chile–garlic paste. Taste and add more to your personal taste, up to 6 tablespoons (although you can add even more than 6 tablespoons if you want). Simmer for 2 to 3 minutes.

3. Ladle the soup into individual bowls and season with the fish sauce, coconut sugar, and lime juice to taste. (Alternatively, you may use any combination of those to suit your own tastes.)

Thai Tomato-Basil Soup

Makes 3 to 4 servings

There are three keys to this recipe: The first is, of course, Thai basil. The second is juicy, ripe tomatoes. The third is coconut cream.

I'd encourage you to avoid conventional supermarket tomatoes, which are usually left to ripen on trucks and often lack sweetness and flavor. That being said, I find even the juiciest, local, in-season, organic tomatoes need a little help in this recipe. After adding the Thai basil and coconut milk and pureeing it all together, give it a taste. It can often be a tad sharp and acidic. And that's where the third key—the coconut cream—comes in. This will instantly mellow things out while simultaneously creating a creamier texture and sweeter flavor. However, when I made it for my roommate, she liked it better without the coconut cream. Go figure. Everyone is different!

Ingredients

5 to 6 large juicy, ripe tomatoes

1 tablespoon olive oil

1 medium onion, coarsely chopped

1 rib celery or 3 ribs Chinese celery, coarsely chopped

1 jalapeño or serrano, seeded and finely chopped

3 to 4 garlic cloves, finely chopped

1 (½-inch) piece fresh ginger, peeled and finely chopped

2 cups chicken bone broth (pages 47-51)

2 tablespoons fish sauce, plus more to taste

1 teaspoon palm sugar, or to taste

Pinch chile powder, plus more to taste

½ cup tightly packed fresh Thai basil leaves

1 (14-ounce) can full-fat coconut milk

1 to 2 cups coconut cream (optional)

Seasonings, to Taste

Fish sauce

Chile powder

Coconut sugar

Fresh Thai basil leaves, coarsely chopped

Fresh lime juice

Directions

1. Peel the skin off the tomatoes by cutting a small *X* on the bottom of each tomato with a knife. Submerge the tomatoes in boiling water for about 15 to 20 seconds. Remove the tomatoes from the boiling water, set them aside until they are cool enough to handle, and peel the skin off. It should easily peel off. Finely chop the tomatoes and set aside.

2. Heat the oil in a large stockpot over medium heat. Add the onion, celery, and jalapeño and sauté for 2 to 3 minutes, until the mixture is fragrant. Add the garlic and ginger and sauté for 1 more minute.

3. Add the tomatoes and cook another 5 to 10 minutes.

4. Add the broth, fish sauce, palm sugar, and chile powder and simmer for 10 to 15 minutes. Taste and add more fish sauce, palm sugar, and chile powder, if needed.

5. Add the Thai basil and coconut milk, stir to combine, and puree with a handheld immersion blender until smooth. (Alternatively, transfer the soup in batches to a regular blender and blend until smooth.)

6. Taste the pureed soup. If desired, add the coconut cream for a creamier texture and slightly sweeter flavor. Add about ½ cup at a time, mixing well, tasting and adding more until the desired consistency and flavor are reached.

7. Ladle the soup into individual bowls and season with the fish sauce, chile powder, coconut sugar, Thai basil, and lime juice to taste. (Alternatively, you may use any combination of those to suit your own tastes.)

Acknowledgments

Thank you to my roommate, Janice, for your patience and understanding as I upended your entire kitchen for long periods during the testing and photographing of the recipes—especially the days I sent strange odors wafting through the house. I promise to never use shrimp paste in your presence ever again.

Thank you to Dwight Beebe for making the wooden photo backgrounds and for the feedback during the many days of recipe testing. I will always remember the expression on your face when you first tasted tom saap.

Thank you to Dan Lohaus for shooting and editing the recipe promo video for the sales page for this book. One day, in a universe far, far away, I am sure you will beat me in cornhole.

Thank you to the team at Archangel Ink, especially Kristie Ledgerwood, for patiently and thoroughly answering all my questions.

Thank you to the tea and coffeehouses of Northampton, Massachusetts, for allowing me to sit in your establishments with nothing but a cup of coffee for hours on end while I wrote this book. In particular, I would like to thank Northampton Coffee, The Roost, Dobra Tea, and Esselon Cafe.

Thank you to Tran's World Food Market in Hadley, Massachusetts, for having an awesome selection of Thai ingredients. I'm not sure I would have written this book without the comfort of knowing that anything I needed was just a short drive away.

Thank you to my parents for your support and encouragement despite the many detours and unconventional paths through which this crazy life has taken me. I will always come home, no matter how far I travel.

And, of course, thank you to Thailand and the many wonderful Thai cooks I met during my travels for your generosity, smiles, and willingness to help, share, and teach—even when language barriers prevented verbal communication. *Korp kun kap*!

Endnotes

1   Barbara O. Rennard et al., "Chicken Soup Inhibits Neutrophil Chemotaxis *In Vitro*," *Chest* 118, no. 4 (2000): 1150–1157, http://dx.doi.org/10.1378/chest.118.4.1150.

2   Sally Fallon Morrell and Kaayla T. Daniel, *Nourishing Broth: An Old-Fashioned Remedy for the Modern World* (New York: Grand Central Life & Style, 2014), 22–23.

3   T. Ohno et al., "Antimicrobial Activity of Essential Oils Against *Helicobacter pylori*.," *Helicobacter* 8, no. 3 (2003): 207–215, https://www.ncbi.nlm.nih.gov/pubmed/12752733.

4   R. N. Okigbo and E. C. Mmeka, "Antimicrobial Effects of Three Tropical Plant Extracts on *Staphylococcus aureus*, *Escherichia coli* and *Candida albicans*," *African Journal of Traditional, Complementary and Alternative Medicines* 5, no. 3 (2008): 226–229, https://www.ncbi.nlm.nih.gov/pmc/articles/PMC2816559/.

5   E. C. Adukwu, S. C. H. Allen, and C. A. Phillips, "The Anti-Biofilm Activity of Lemongrass (*Cymbopogon flexuosus*) and Grapefruit (*Citrus paradisi*) Essential Oils Against Five Strains of *Staphylococcus aureus*," *Journal of Applied Microbiology* 113, no. 5 (2012): 1217–1227, doi:10.1111/j.1365-2672.2012.05418.x.

6   B. Cde Silva et al., "Antifungal Activity of the Lemongrass Oil and Citral Against Candida Spp.," *Brazilian Journal of Infectious Diseases* 12, no. 1 (2008): 63–66, https://www.ncbi.nlm.nih.gov/pubmed/18553017.

7   Tamonud Modak and Abhilash Mukhopadhaya, "Effects of Citral, a Naturally Occurring Antiadipogenic Molecule, on an Energy-Intense Diet Model of Obesity," *Indian Journal of Pharmacology* 43, no. 3 (2011): 300–305, doi:10.4103/0253-7613.81515.

8   T. F. Bachiega and J. M. Sforcin, "Lemongrass and Citral Effect on Cytokines Production by Murine Macrophages," *Journal of Ethnopharmacology* 137, no. 1 (2011): 909–913, doi:10.1016/j.jep.2011.07.021.

9   C. A. Costa et al., "Cholesterol Reduction and Lack of Genotoxic or Toxic Effects in Mice After Repeated 21-Day Oral Intake of Lemongrass (*Cymbopogon citratus*) Essential Oil," *Food and Chemical Toxicology* 49, no. 9 (2011): 2268–2272, doi:10.1016/j.fct.2011.06.025.

10 Jirawan Oonmetta-aree et al., "Antimicrocrobial Properties and Action of Galangal (*Alpinia galanga* Linn.) on *Staphylococcus aureus*," *LWT – Food Science and Technology* 39, no. 10 (2006): 1214–1220, http://dx.doi.org/10.1016/j.lwt.2005.06.015.

11 A. M. Janssen and J. J. C. Scheffer, "Acetoxychavicol Acetate, an Antifungal Component of *Alpinia galanga* 1," *Planta Medica* 51, no. 6 (1986): 507–511, doi:10.1055/s-2007-969577.

12   D. Bendjeddou, K. Lalaoui, and D. Satta, "Immunostimulating Activity of the Hot Water–Soluble Polysaccharide Extracts of *Anacyclus pyrethrum*, *Alpinia galanga* and *Citrullus colocynthis*," *Journal of Ethnopharmacology* 88, nos. 2–3 (2003): 155–160, https://www.ncbi.nlm.nih.gov/pubmed/12963136.

13   Mosa-Al-Reza Hadjzadeh et al., "The Effects of Aqueous Extract of *Alpinia galangal* on Gastric Cancer Cells (AGS) and L929 Cells in Vitro," *Iranian Journal of Cancer Prevention* 7, no. 3 (2014): 142–146, https://www.ncbi.nlm.nih.gov/pmc/articles/PMC4171825/.

14   Fah Chueahongthong et al., "Cytotoxic Effects of Crude Kaffir Lime (*Citrus hystrix*, DC.) Leaf Fractional Extracts on Leukemic Cell Lines," *Journal of Medicinal Plants Research* 5, no. 14 (2011): 3097–3105, http://www.academicjournals.org/article/article1380622014_Chueahongthong%20et%20al.pdf.

15   Woro Anindito Sri Tunjung et al., "Anti-Cancer Effect of Kaffir Lime (*Citrus hystrix* DC) Leaf Extract in Cervical Cancer and Neuroblastoma Cell Lines," *Procedia Chemistry* 14 (2015): 465–468, http://dx.doi.org/10.1016/j.proche.2015.03.062.

16   Tapanee Hongratanaworakit and Gerhard Buchbauer, "Chemical Composition and Stimulating Effect of *Citrus hystrix* Oil on Humans," *Flavour and Fragrance Journal* 22, no. 5 (2007): 443–449, https://www.researchgate.net/publication/230328079_Chemical_composition_and_stimulating_effect_of_Citrus_hystrix_oil_on_humans.

17   N. Kooltheat et al., "Kaffir Lime Leaves Extract Inhibits Biofilm Formation by *Streptococcus mutans*," *Nutrition* 32, no. 4 (2016): 486–490, doi:10.1016/j.nut.2015.10.010.

18   A. Tawatsin et al., "Repellency of Volatile Oils from Plants Against Three Mosquito Vectors," *Journal of Vector Ecology* 26, no. 1 (2001): 76–82, https://www.ncbi.nlm.nih.gov/pubmed/11469188.

19   Chris Kresser, "RHR: Is the Glycemic Index Useful?" *Chris Kresser* (blog), February 26, 2015, https://chriskresser.com/is-the-glycemic-index-useful/.

20   John Casey, "The Hidden Ingredient That Can Sabotage Your Diet," WebMD, accessed November 22, 2016, http://www.webmd.com/diet/features/the-hidden-ingredient-that-can-sabotage-your-diet#1.

21   Kristen Michaelis, "Coconut Sugar Is Sustainable," *Food Renegade* (blog), accessed December 1, 2016, http://www.foodrenegade.com/coconut-sugar-sustainable/.

22   Jessica Prentice, *Full Moon Feast: Food and the Hunger for Connection* (White River Junction, VT: Chelsea Green Publishing, 2012), 35.

23   "Digestive Diseases Statistics for the United States," NIH National Institute of Diabetes and Digestive and Kidney Diseases, last modified November 2014, https://www.niddk.nih.gov/health-information/health-statistics/Pages/digestive-diseases-statistics-for-the-united-states.aspx.

24   "20 Harmful Effects of Caffeine," Caffeine Informer, last modified February 1, 2017, http://www.caffeineinformer.com/harmful-effects-of-caffeine.

25   Magdalena Donejko et al., "Influence of Caffeine and Hyaluronic Acid on Collagen Biosynthesis in Human Skin Fibroblasts," *Drug Design, Development and Therapy* 8 (2014): 1923–1928, doi:10.2147/DDDT.S69791.

26 "Insomnia: Studies Suggest Calcium and Magnesium Effective," Medical News Today, September 8, 2009, http://www.medicalnewstoday.com/releases/163169.php.

27 Wataru Yamadera et al., "Glycine Ingestion Improves Subjective Sleep Quality in Human Volunteers, Correlating with Polysomnographic Changes," *Sleep and Biological Rhythms* 5, no. 2 (2007): 126–131, doi:10.1111/j.1479-8425.2007.00262.x.

28 J. K. Grover and S. P. Yadav, "Pharmacological Actions and Potential Uses of *Momordica charantia*: A Review," *Journal of Ethnopharmacology* 93, no. 1 (2004): 123–132, doi:10.1016/j.jep.2004.03.035.

Made in the USA
Middletown, DE
27 May 2017